INGA

INGA
MY STORY

Va'aiga Tuigamala

with

Myan Subrayan

First published by Penguin Group (NZ), 2009
Copyright © Va'aiga Tuigamala, 2009, 2011

Published by Hope2Overcome 2011

The right of Myan Subrayan to be identified as the author of this work
in terms of section 96 of the Copyright Act 1994 is hereby asserted.

All photographs are from Va'aiga Tuigamala's personal collection,
unless otherwise credited.

ISBN 978 0 143 20355 1

A catalogue record for this book is available
from the National Library of New Zealand.

Contents

To my wife, Daphne, and my children, Jordan, Vaise, Salote and Silika. Thank you for helping me learn some of the greatest lessons in life, as a husband and father.

I really appreciate you for loving me just as I am.

With all my love, Dad.

To Keith Mills, a true legend of Wigan (7 May 1944-16 April 2012)

The Man in the Glass

Anonymous

When you get what you want in your struggle for self
And the world makes you king for a day,
Just go to the mirror and look at yourself
And see what that man has to say.

For it isn't your father or mother or wife
Whose judgement upon you must pass.
The fellow whose verdict counts most in your life
Is the one staring back from the glass.

Some people say you're a straight-shooting chum
And think you're a wonderful guy.
But the man in the glass says you're only a bum
If you can't look him straight in the eye.

He's the fellow to please but don't forget about the rest,
For he's with you clear to the end.
And you've passed your most difficult test
If the man in the glass is your friend.

You may fool the whole world down the pathway of years
And get pats on the back as you pass.
But your final reward will be heartache and tears
If you've cheated the man in the glass.

Foreword

I recall at the beginning of 1994 Inga making news as a big name signing for Wigan. For us players it didn't really matter a lot. At that time Wigan were full of other big name players at the club, so Inga was not treated any differently, as he was a star amongst many other stars.

Whilst he may have been known as the All Black, Inga the Winger when he arrived, our coach, Graham West, made the crucial decision to move him off the wing into centre. That's when I believe we saw Inga's world class and when he was at his best. I must say that it was a brilliant move by Graham because with Jason Robinson, Martin Offiah and Inga in the team we had three world class wingers. Graham wanted to incorporate all of them in the starting line-up, but the reality was there was only space for two wingers.

At centre Inga would have more of a chance to show off his skills and off course the crowd favourite: him knocking opponents off the ball. We had a really formidable back line with Jason Robinson and Inga operating from the right and Gary Connelly and Martin Offiah from the left.

It was not just Inga's power or brute strength that he possessed to run over the opposition that made him a great player, he was also very skilful. He had a deft touch and was quite nimble on his feet, and with ball in hand this made him a really special player. I can recall he had a late shimmy, when combined with his already mentioned skills, more than often got the job done. He was also unselfish and created the space to put someone else into a gap. Having played some basketball with him I observed from where he got his "soft hand skills." He was fantastic even at basketball.

Inga later mentions how he tried to pick on me at his first training session at Wigan, singling out the "small white boy." I admit when you are smaller than the rest, everyone wants to pick on you, which is something that I got used to and learnt very well to handle (as you will read about later). Wigan was a professional team in 1990 and it was our full time job to play rugby. The fad of protein shakes and vitamin supplements was very prevalent with us even back in 1990.

Despite the super star status that came with Inga as a high profile All Black when he arrived at Wigan, he displayed immense humility. As you will read in Chapter 4, he wasn't at the top of the tree but he had the discipline and work ethic that did eventually get him to the top. He further shares candidly on how unfit he was by Rugby League standards, but all credit to him as he worked really hard to improve. In all honesty he did improve very well, so much so that in the next 94/95 season we saw this great player explode onto the Rugby League scene. Chris Butler our conditioning coach who coached 400 and 800 metre runners worked with Inga, and played a big part with Inga's fitness and conditioning. As captain of the team I used to be on Inga's case often, and push him at training. We used to also enjoy sparring with each other. He packed a mean punch which I felt once when he got me on my ear. The ringing went on for quite some time.

In the preseason training for that 94/95 season we were put through our paces up Haigh Hall Hill. Here you found out very soon where you were at, in terms of fitness. For anyone that's been there you know it's the last bit, when you get up to the gates, it's about 250 metres long and quite steep, which is a real killer. It was very taxing, and here that Inga first struggled in his early days at Wigan. But later on he 'owned' that hill.

All of this pre-season training eventually paid off, and from that 94/95 season onwards we got the best from him.

Away from rugby he had a warmth that drew people to him. Even though I was older than him, I would often go to him for advice. He was mature, wiser and someone that I looked up to. In times of distress you could not have asked for anyone better as a friend, as he was always there for you. He was a man of strong faith but never forced it on anyone. Many of us guys used language that was not very decent, but whenever Inga was around we respected him so much that we curbed it in his presence. He never asked us to do so, but such was the respect he had earned amongst the team. I used to joke that Inga was the type of guy that any dad would have wanted to marry their daughter.

When he moved on from Wigan to Newcastle, it was good to learn that he took what he had learnt from his time with us, and imparted some of it at Newcastle Falcons. They went on to achieve much success with Inga as a central figure in that team, as Rob Andrew shares. The role model Inga became to Jason Robinson, he also became to Jonny Wilkinson. As you read on I am sure you will get to know why these guys embraced him as such!

Shaun Edwards
Former Wigan Warriors Captain and Head Coach for London Wasps
Current Defence coach for Wales Rugby

Introduction

'Inga, your son thinks his daddy is dead.'

These are not the sort of words you want to hear from your wife – especially when you are thousands of miles apart, travelling around on another continent. You want to hear comforting talk about the exciting new things your little kids are getting up to. But those were the very words I heard over the telephone, while I was on the 1993 northern hemisphere tour with the All Blacks. It was a really sobering moment for me and gave me quite a shock. But that was exactly how it happened at the time, and it's also how I have planned this book – to be as honest as I can possibly be as I share with you from my perspective the truth of what was and is going on in my life.

Since my last biography in 1993 – in which I was described

as 'the skinny island kid with the afro' – a lot has happened and changed in my life. For one thing, you'll see from a glance at my photo on the cover of this book that both my 'skinny' and 'afro' days are well and truly gone. The earlier book spoke a lot about my achievements on the rugby field. Well, I can assuredly say to you that much water has passed under the bridge since then. I like to think that I am more mature than I was at that time. There is definitely so much more to tell than what has already been said.

At the very outset when I sat down with the publishing team that has helped make this book possible, I made my intentions very clear. This was not going to be just another book about a sporting 'has-been'. Because, let's face it, that's part of the reality of what I currently am – a 'has-been' rugby player. No, what you are going to read in these pages is a 'no holds barred' version of my life after my playing days with the All Blacks. Don't despair, though, as I do share some of my experiences from when I first donned the All Black jersey. Those memorable days laid the platform for so much of my later life and I could never forget them.

Even now, I am still fondly known as 'Inga the Winger' to many people. When they call me by that name, I politely acknowledge them. But the reality is that I am no longer just 'Inga the Winger' – I am so much more than that person, as you will find out for yourself as you read on. I have moved ahead from my playing days, and do not live in the past – just as we should all learn from the past and move on.

It should be a rudder that guides us
and not an anchor that weighs us down
(Warren Wiersbe).

Even staying where you are isn't good enough. Consider what happens to stagnant water – it can become pretty unpleasant. You get the point? You need to be moving forward in life all the time. And that's exactly what I like to do – move forward!

Don't get me wrong – I won't ever resent my playing days. I have always counted it a privilege to have stepped onto the field for some of the world's great teams. On an international level, no one can ever take away the pride that I got from playing for the All Blacks. On the other hand, there were limitations that came with wearing the 'black jersey'. It was these limitations that made me consider the alternatives available to me at that time. As you read on, you will find out what these options were, and more importantly, why I chose them. You will also hear from some of my former team-mates – individuals such as Apollo Perelini, Jason Robinson, Jonny Wilkinson, Rob Andrew, Martin Offiah and many more – along with others associated with me from my playing era. I will take you through my travels from New Zealand to Europe and then back home again, with the odd side trip thrown in for good measure.

Sixteen years of my life have passed since those 'glory' days. This is my opportunity to share with you what has happened between then and now. Hopefully, you will come to see that there is more to Inga Tuigamala than my former accomplishments on the sports field, while at the same time learn the answers to some of the following questions:

- What were my reasons for leaving the All Blacks and New Zealand to play for Wigan?
- Why did I switch from Wigan to Newcastle, from league back to union?
- What was life like in the northern hemisphere?
- Why return to New Zealand when I had so much going for me in Europe?
- What on earth inspired me to become an undertaker?

The book you hold in your hands is not just my attempt to answer such questions and many more besides. It will also give you the 'inside scoop'. By describing what was happening in my life back then, I hope to present the background knowledge and insight to what was going through my mind prior to making those life-changing decisions.

Prior to my introduction to the game, the average rugby winger was a slim, lightweight fellow. I changed all that. I have never been a person to accept the status quo in my life either, and that's what people have come to expect from me. This book is no different. It is my life and my story – as authorised by me. So what you can expect from this book is what you have come to expect from me, Inga: to be honest and true and *unexpected*! I invite you to join me on this no-holds-barred journey through my life.

Va'aiga Tuigamala
August 2009

1.

The Journey Begins

A journey of a thousand miles
begins with a single step.

Lao-tzu

I t was heartbreaking for me to hear those words from my wife; the words spoken to her by my eldest son, Jordan, who was around three years old at the time: 'Is my daddy dead?' And who could blame him? Because he hadn't seen me around for such a long time, his little three-year-old mind had deduced that I was no longer alive.

It was taxing being away from home on those international tours of duty with the All Blacks. Not just physically, but more. It took its toll on us emotionally as well. There were also the domestic games away from Auckland that I spent apart from my family too. Little Jordan's words rang out in my head like a shotgun blast. It was worse than the feeling I got from missing a tackle that could have stopped the opposition scoring. Even worse than losing a big game. It was a total reality check for me.

Time away from family and loved ones is one of the many sacrifices that professional sportsmen and sportswomen have to make. Back then it was taken for granted that it was just one of the demands that the game required of us. Believe me, whether you're married or not, it is never an easy choice to make. It's tough being away from your loved ones, and doubly tough when you are so far from them travelling in a foreign land. That's why my phone bill on one of my Europe tours was more than three thousand dollars.

Rugby still hadn't become a professional sport back in my playing days. The game, sad to say, didn't provide well financially for us players. While I thank God for having been given the honour of playing for the All Blacks, it was pretty much only that pride in wearing the black jersey that fended off many tempting initial offers from league scouts to switch codes. Despite travelling and staying in class and style, being pampered with many luxuries, the truth was that when I got back it was an altogether different story. Being an All Black did not meet the needs in my home.

The cold, hard fact awaiting me when I got home was that at that time of our lives my wife Daphne and I were living out the back of my mum's house, sleeping on makeshift beds on a concrete slab in the garage. I was grateful to Mum for the roof she offered my family and me, but I knew that was definitely not the way to continue providing for my wife and kids. They deserved better. It was time for me to consider other options – options that required me to wear not just my playing cap, but my husband and father caps as well.

Hearing Jordan's words from my wife also made me reflect on how selfish I had been as a little boy. It brought to mind the self-centred demands I placed on my own dad when I was growing up, and in particular an occasion when I was about nine or ten years old and had travelled away with my team to another little West Auckland town by the name of Kumeu.

Just as I had noticed the other kids' dads doing at their kids' games, I always longed for Dad to turn up and watch me play. It used to crush me when I saw all the other dads cheering their kids on from the sidelines. I used to take it out on Mum:

> 'When's Dad going to watch *me* play?
> Will he ever make the time for *me*?'

Mum never let Dad down and explained that he was working and couldn't make it. You see, my immature mind simply did not understand the difficulty of Dad's situation. Only later did I come to understand it: it was tough going for my parents to provide for their fourteen children.

When Mum and Dad brought us to New Zealand from Samoa in 1974, they came with the hope that this country would offer us a better life. Along with the majority of Pacific Island migrants to New Zealand, their focus was on three main things:

1. Get a job. It didn't matter what job – cleaning toilets, the freezing works, road works – any job would do!
2. Put food on the table for the family.
3. Buy a house.

My dad's responsibilities far outweighed my expectation of him to turn up at my rugby games. Or to be there for me at night to tuck me in and read a bedtime story. I couldn't comprehend his absences at the time. All I saw was my dad not being there for me at my games. Why couldn't he be like the other kids' dads? They were at their games. They read to their kids at night and tucked them into bed. Surely it couldn't be that hard for him to do the same. Couldn't he at least get time off to come watch me play once in a while?

However, all my resentments about Dad's fathering skills were to change drastically for me on the way home from that game in Kumeu. I had scored three or four tries and we had won the game. Even now I recall how, even though we had won, I was angry with Dad for not turning up. On the trip home I was sitting at the back of the family Holden station wagon sulking. All of a sudden, I heard Mum exclaim, 'What on earth is he doing?' There was Dad walking along the side of the road. Mum stopped and he got in. He had managed to get off early from work and was on his way to watch me play. The problem was that no one had told him the bus only went up to Massey and not all the way to Kumeu. It stopped short about four kilometres from where I was playing. I couldn't believe how wrong I had been about my dad. He had sacrificed and made the effort to come and see me play. All my feelings of anger gave way to remorse, sympathy and guilt. I became ashamed of myself and began to cry. After that day, I learnt to appreciate him much more.

My dad, Va'aiga Lealuga Tuigamala I, passed away on the 24th of April 1981, just two years later. I loved my father. Even though he could not spend all the time with me that I had wanted him to, I understood the reasons why. I am forever grateful for the decision Dad made to bring us over from Samoa to New Zealand too. After all, it was that choice that made it possible for me to achieve my dream and be here telling my life story all these years later.

Accordingly, I made it my priority as a father to learn from my dad's example; to try as hard as possible to provide for my family as he did for us. Moreover, I wanted to make sure that my own children had the reassurance that their father would be there for them. I didn't want them to have to feel the pain I did when my dad was not around. So I made a commitment always to be there for them.

I was once told that the way a child spells love is

$$T - I - M - E.$$

In other words, they value the time that you spend with them more than anything else. All the video games, chocolates and gifts in the world cannot substitute for the precious moments you spend with them. In the long run,

it's your *presence* more than your *presents*
that matters to your kids.

Fast-forward to being away from my family on All Blacks tours and the financial hardships we faced and it puts the decision I made to switch codes to play in Wigan in perspective.

The opportunity to play rugby league for Wigan offered me the chance to have the best of both my worlds: to be able to play the sport that I loved and have my family there with me to enjoy and celebrate it together. On top of that, my salary from Wigan meant the financial woes I used to face back in New Zealand would be a thing of the past. Many people said that it was the money that lured me away from New Zealand. I would be lying if I said that was untrue. Yes! Money was definitely part of the decision, but not all of it. Along with the money factor was the reality of our family's uncertain future at that time in my life.

Of course, none of the newspaper headlines focused on our difficult financial circumstances. No, most of them were about the huge salary I would be getting paid. It was my responsibility as a father and husband to provide for my family. That was the main decider – that and the fact that my long absences from home due to playing rugby union meant to my three-year-old that I was 'dead'. When I look around at the pressures of this world that are being placed on families, I shudder. I shudder to think how many parents are similarly 'dead' to their kids. Just as with me, I don't doubt there may be compelling reasons they are not there to spend time with them. But is it really any wonder that we have so many children in today's society getting into trouble with authority?

The importance of family is something that was instilled in me by my parents. This is why I have chosen to dedicate this book to my wife and kids. May it be an inspiration to all parents to never take for granted the privilege they have been given by The Almighty to raise their children – and not just raise them, but do it the correct way by setting an example and being a good role model for them. There is a lovely saying that speaks volumes to us as parents:

'Children shut their ears to advice
and open their eyes to example.'

In other words, no amount of talking can substitute for parents living out and modelling the behaviour and conduct they want from their children. That's what I want to be for my children – a role model for all the things that I want to see in them.

While I don't claim in any way to be the perfect father, I always try to do my best. The same dedication and commitment I gave on the field, I give to raising my family. Why? Because they are infinitely more precious and valuable than all the accolades I received for my exploits on the pitch. Remember: in the long run it's your presence more than your presents that matters to your kids.

2.

New Beginnings

It is choice – not chance –
that determines your destiny.

Jean Nidetch

I can confidently say that the move to Wigan to take up my first professional contract was the start of something truly significant in my life. It was a time when I had to stretch as a person and a time when Inga the Winger actually grew up. I believe it was my coming of age as a player, a husband and a father. Although there were many tears shed while saying our final goodbyes to extended family and friends as we departed Auckland International Airport in January 1994, this defining moment laid the foundation for my future as well as that of my family.

When we left New Zealand it was summer and therefore we were clad in our typical summer clothes for the flight over. What a climate shock to arrive in England smack in the middle of a snowy winter! During the drive from Manchester Airport, I remember thinking back to the decision my parents had made in 1974. Now, some twenty years later, I found myself doing exactly the same thing – migrating to another country for the prospect of a better future for our kids. It was a real step of faith into the unknown. Add in the cultural differences we faced, raising a young family, pressures of a new game, the media, fans, and so on, and you pretty much get the picture of what we were up against. Through all the adjustments and challenges we would soon face adapting to life in a new land, we would be able to empathise more with what my own parents would have experienced when they first arrived in New Zealand.

My time in England brought me many successes. I like to describe it as 'an experience and a half'. But before these successes came, much growth was first required of me. Outside the comfort zone of my wider family and friends, secure in their unquestioned level of support, in England I had to stand up and look after my own family. However, I was ready to face the challenges ahead and not afraid to try. It is my firm belief that we only begin to achieve growth when we stretch ourselves, going beyond what we may have previously achieved or are familiar with. As the saying goes:

'People are like rubber bands, they are most effective when they are stretched.'

I shudder to think of what the outcome could have been for us had I not taken that opportunity. Looking around me now, I see the many challenges that union players of my time face because the code was not professional back then. They played for the love of the game, but regrettably that love was unrequited when it came to taking care of their financial needs.

People like to think that I was lucky. I don't agree.

I don't believe in luck, although I do believe
in wishing my opponents the best of luck
before a game

– then I go out and play so that they don't get any of it during my watch! What others may call luck, I prefer to call effort. As my former mentor Don Oliver liked to say:

'Luck only comes in when talent runs out.'

In life, success largely comes down to the choices we make. It was *choice* – not *chance* – that determined my destiny. I must admit, faced with the decision of moving or not, at the time it seemed like a hard choice for Daphne and I to make. We were torn between staying within our comfortable known boundaries in New Zealand, or stepping out of our comfort zone into the unknown and unfamiliar with no safety net.

It was common knowledge by that time that I was being hunted down by league scouts and that some lucrative offers were being made. After I declined an earlier offer from Wigan in 1993, I was invited to appear on the *Holmes* TV show where I made it clear that money had never been a priority in my life. My reason for turning the offer down was that I felt it was not right at that time. At the end of the show, Paul Holmes commented on how impressed he was by my honesty. Throughout my life, it has always been my aim to be honest.

While I'm on the subject, I also remember my good friend

the sports journalist Murray Deaker dedicating one of his television shows to highlighting the predicament that we were facing in 1993. The show opened with the song 'Should I Stay or Should I Go?' by The Clash. The question then posed to the viewers was: 'What should Inga do?' According to Murray, the response was overwhelming. It was also encouraging to note that so many understood my responsibility to my family rather than to rugby only. Over the years, Murray and I have become close friends, even though he was one of my earlier critics for leaving New Zealand to play overseas.

Later, Murray confided to me his reasons for feeling that I would not make it in England. They were mainly related to my Pacific Island background. He was genuinely concerned that not having my extended family around would be to my detriment and make my time there unenjoyable. In his own words, I would be 'homesick and back very soon'. Now, when I remind him of this prediction, he laughs and admits that he was pleasantly surprised that I proved him wrong and ended up staying for nine years. What surprised him even more was that I was able to survive without my favourite Pacific Island food, taro, for that entire length of time. (What Murray didn't know was that we were able to get most of our Pacific Island food at the West Indian markets over there.)

However, Wigan was not the only club that was chasing after me; other offers were on the table as well. Much interest was shown in signing me by Australian league clubs also. Plus, I was torn between these opportunities and the genuine enjoyment and pleasure I got from playing for the All Blacks. The dilemma we faced was: Do we stay or go? And if we do, then where do we go and which club do I choose? Some vital choices needed to be made and I am forever grateful for the advice I received at that crucial time from men I considered to be wise. Their guidance helped to make clear a lot of things for us. More than just their advice, I was taken aback by their genuine concern for me and my family. It surpassed their personal interest in me remaining in New Zealand. I feel compelled to single out two of these individuals for particular praise. The first is Laurie Mains.

Laurie Mains
Former All Blacks coach
'Laurie Mains really drilled the fear of God into you.'

Towards the end of my last days with the All Blacks I was grateful to Laurie Mains for his advice and support. He was very aware of the offers from league that I was getting and also understood the considerable pressure that I was being subjected to by them. The great thing about Laurie is that he did not suggest that the league move was wrong. He advised me that I should carefully consider all my options and not rush into any decisions; that I should consult many people and more importantly consider my family. Laurie also made me seriously think about the decision I had to make and he did this by raising a lot of pertinent issues. The main issue being how I would be able to adjust to being away from family. Laurie also assured me that he had plans for me in 1994 with the All Blacks.

His encouraging words helped ease the pressure. Laurie was a man who I had a huge amount of respect and admiration for. On numerous occasions he met with me and just talked everything through. He really took the time and showed me that he was a very different man to what I had previously perceived him to be. Until that time, like so many of the other players, I was fearful of him. As a coach, Laurie Mains really drilled the fear of God into you. His methods were intense, but it was all geared to bringing out the best in his players. Now this person of authority of whom I had grown to have a respectful fear was showing me a side of his personality I had not seen before as a player. Laurie was more concerned about my and my family's personal welfare. He didn't have to take the time to be concerned, but he chose to do so. He was the All Blacks coach and not our counsellor, but he made the effort to find out what I was really going through in my personal life.

As I have already indicated, my personal circumstances were not something that I was proud to divulge – living out of a garage and struggling for employment and experiencing financial problems. Yet I am forever grateful to Laurie Mains for the time and effort he invested towards helping me with his wise words of advice. It really meant a lot to me at the time as it made it a little easier for me to consider my various options.

The other person who deserves an accolade is Kevin Roberts, CEO of Lion Nathan at the time. He was passionate about business and very successful in his own right. Presently he is residing in New York where he is CEO of Saatchi & Saatchi worldwide. While I was still with the All Blacks, Kevin was able to give me a much-needed start in New Zealand. I was really appreciative of the employment opportunity with Pepsi-Cola International that he made possible whereby I became the 'face' of Pepsi in New Zealand for a short time in the early 1990s. Since then, we have been really great friends.

More than just giving me my major employment break in New Zealand, Kevin Roberts – like Laurie Mains – offered me good counsel and advice regarding my offers. I remember going over with Daphne to see Kevin to discuss the finer points of my Wigan contract. He didn't tell me whether I should go or not, but gave me wonderful advice all the same. At turning points like these, it is so important to have the right people speaking into your life and looking out for your best interests. Kevin was another such friend to me.

Kevin Roberts

Former CEO of Lion Nathan, which controlled Pepsi in New Zealand

'Inga was probably the world's worst bad debt collector!'

'I first met Inga at Laurie Mains' request. He told me that Inga was the most powerful wing force he'd ever seen after John Kirwan and that he was an integral part of the All Blacks going forward. At that time, Inga was young, inexperienced, shy and – as I recall it – living in pretty average circumstances.

'As part of a large family, he and Daphne were temporarily residing in a garage conversion at home, although I'm not sure how converted it really was. He was also employed by an Auckland car dealer collecting bad debts. Inga was probably the world's worst bad debt collector! Inevitably, he ended up listening to the sob stories, giving them a pass, or even trying to help them out himself – not really what you're looking for in a debt collector. At that time, Lion Nathan was a primary sponsor of the All Blacks through Steinlager and we had just successfully concluded a deal with PepsiCo International to bottle and market Pepsi brands in New Zealand and Australia. I was looking for real-life ways to make Pepsi part of the community – a difficult task given the historical dominance of Coca-Cola in this country.

'I had been very impressed with Inga's personal qualities, his sense of fun and his magical touch and empathy with youth. His Christian values shone through and his sheer exuberance, size (and clumsiness) made kids feel that he was one of them. We were positioning Pepsi as the "Choice of a New Generation" and I could think of nobody in New Zealand who represented those values more than Inga Tuigamala. I asked him if he would represent us in the community and become the face and role model for Pepsi in this country. His qualities of fun, optimism, joy and empathy with youth made him a natural ambassador for the brand.

'I'll never forget the look on his face when I offered him the job at my house in Remuera, Auckland, and I showed him the car he would be given. An all-black, pumped-up Rav 4 with personalised INGA number plate. He was like a little kid and couldn't wait to get to work. Michael Jones joined him and the two made a formidable pairing at schools, sports events, and everywhere in the local community where youth gathered. This was great for Pepsi, great for the All Blacks, great for Laurie and, I think, a real turning point for Inga. He found he could really make a difference when backed by a strong brand and he loved being part of something. Pepsi was a maverick, renegade guerrilla movement against the well-entrenched Coke and I think Inga really enjoyed this aspect of the job.

'From there, Inga and I developed a lifetime friendship which burns strongly to this day. At that time, I had a boxing ring and a squash court in my house. I couldn't keep Inga out of the ring, and both my kids, Ben and Daniel, had great times in there with him. It certainly put them off boxing for life! Inga and I used to play squash regularly, and if you thought he was potent on the wing, you can imagine him on the T in a squash court! The big black bus wasn't the most agile of opponents but he was certainly difficult to manoeuvre around.

'On the topic of Wigan, Inga and Daphne came to me at Portland Road one day and told me of the offer. He was clearly torn between his commitments to New Zealand, the All Blacks, family, and his desire to give Daphne a life she never imagined, make a better life for his kids, and test himself as an athlete. He poured his heart out for over an hour. I listened, told him that you make the big decisions with your heart and the small ones with your head: this was a big decision and he should follow his heart. From there, I asked him to take a look at his life in New Zealand and what the future held for him here. Because of his Pacific Island roots and family circumstances, I felt it would be difficult for him to give Daphne and his kids the best possible choice. The extended family syndrome sucks up most of the resources of the individual for the community. This has good points, but it also has more difficult areas, particularly when one man is driven by ambition and growth and the rest of the community are driven more by the need for security. It can mean that that one man's ambition gets submerged and never realised.

'I come from Lancaster in the North of England, 25 miles from Wigan, and was able to tell Inga how friendly and welcoming folks in Lancashire are. I also told him how he would be given the opportunity to be the best he could be and to provide Daphne and the kids with a new life experience they could never have in New Zealand. From a rugby point of view, it seemed to me that he wasn't built for league. Adapting his body to the different demands of rugby league would be another challenge for him to overcome.

'Three hours later, without attempting to reach any con-
clusion, Inga and Daphne left and we spoke again a couple
of times before he told me that he had decided to make the
move. He made the decision in conjunction with Daphne,
having listened I guess to a couple of people but then having
made his own mind up. It really turned out to be a fantastic
decision for Inga, his family and sport – although we certainly
missed him in New Zealand with the All Blacks.'

*Kevin was right that debt collecting was not one of my fortes.
You can imagine how glad I was that he was able to give me
the Pepsi role.*

There were many other people who were important in my life
and who I spoke to about my offers, such as siblings and close
friends. But I still remember very clearly the time I went to see
my mum. I had not included her in the initial panel of advisors
as I knew she wouldn't be keen on the thought of me leaving
her to live on the other side of the world. When I did pluck up
the courage to see her, I apologised profusely for not including
her amongst the first people I had gone to for advice.

My mother's response startled me. Here I was expecting
her to tell me that I was making the wrong decision in leaving
New Zealand, but I soon learnt that I had totally misjudged her.
I vividly remember her words of wisdom to me, which I still
cherish to this very day:

'Son, sometimes there comes a time in a man's life
when he has to give up the things that he enjoys
to do the things that are more important.'

Even though in Mum's heart she wished we wouldn't
leave, she didn't allow her emotions to cloud her judgement.
She appreciated that for her son and his family to have an
opportunity to secure some financial support and broaden their
horizons and outlook in life, I had to move with the Wigan
contract. Mum knew in her heart that she couldn't hold on to
us any longer.

My final game for the All Blacks was against the Barbarians
on our 1993 tour of Europe, at Cardiff Arms Park. I can
remember preparing for this, my last appearance for the ABs,
with mixed thoughts and was really glad that I managed to mark
my departure by scoring a try. However, it was strange for me as
I couldn't really celebrate that as my last try or appearance for
the All Blacks. This was because I'd been advised not to disclose
anything of the contract that I'd accepted from Wigan prior to
taking the field in that test.

I remember the occasion vividly because although I knew it
was to be my last game in the black jersey as we ran out onto the
park, of course none of the other players knew. I was thinking
that it would be really nice to go out on a high note in my last
appearance for the All Blacks. This is why I remember that try
so well. When I was given the ball early, I seized the opportunity
with both hands. I had a bit of space. Scott Gibbs of Wales, a
great friend of mine, was playing at centre for the Baa-Baas, and
I thought if I could only manage to squeak past him I could

get to the tryline. I can't begin to tell you what a relief it was to get over that line in my last game for the 'men in black'. I did it for my family and my country. Shortly afterwards it was announced that I'd signed a lucrative four-year contract to play rugby league for Wigan.

My decision to play in England brought with it the much-expected criticism. By that time as an All Black I was pretty much used to copping flak. Even before I actually became an All Black I'd received my fair share. Such as this classic one: 'With a name like Tuigamala, you'll never make it to be an All Black – you're probably better changing it to Smith.'

Playing for the All Blacks, I'd found myself in the media spotlight quite often. With my switch to league, the spotlight trained on me became even brighter. Much was being written and said, including predictions that I was making a big mistake by switching codes and moving to England. Those that know me will understand that I am not one to be easily swayed by what others think or say about me. I have what some consider the perfect antidote to criticism – thick skin. My advice to others is to not let the negative things that others say dampen your spirit in the pursuit of your dreams. It has been said that

adversity causes some men to break,
others to break records
(William A. Ward).

On that score, let me just say that there were a few records I did break in England despite enduring some tough times initially. A major one was breaking the transfer fee record for joining Newcastle in 1997.

I know for sure that had I got cold feet about my big move and allowed my fear of the unknown to dominate and cloud my better judgement, all the success that flowed from that move would not have been achieved. It is fear that is frequently responsible for scaring us off from realising our true potential. If we fail to overcome that fear, it will rob us of many great things. In fact, I consider fear to be such a major barrier to someone aspiring to their full potential that I will talk about it a bit more in the next chapter.

3.

Fear is Just an Illusion

Every time we choose safety, we reinforce fear.

Cheri Huber

On reflection, I am very glad that I didn't allow fear to stand in my way of moving to England. Had I done so, I believe that I would have lost out on many great things. Someone once showed me the following acronym on fear that I think is pretty revealing:

False   **E**vidence   **A**ppearing   **R**eal

Quite simply, fear is one of the number one reasons why people don't achieve all of which they are capable. Confronted with situations that seem bigger than ourselves, we are prone to become overwhelmed and afraid. However, in the inspirational words of Sir Edmund Hillary:

'It's not the mountain we conquer, but ourselves.'

Our very own Sir Ed achieved something unprecedented. No one before had successfully climbed Mt Everest. He could have listened to the naysayer who tried to put him down because they felt it was too hard a task to accomplish. But he didn't. He pressed on. We can learn a lot from Sir Ed, to face our fears and challenges head-on and never retreat.

Likewise, without in any way comparing my achievement to Hillary's, I'm glad I didn't allow my fear of the unknown get in the way of making the move to Wigan. In hindsight, I can appreciate how that move not only opened many doors for me in my career, but also gave many other Pacific Island players the encouragement and confidence to follow in my footsteps, as a number of people acknowledge in these pages.

Let me share with you some insightful words that speak the truth about what happens when we overcome our fears and the liberation it brings not only to us, but others as well:

Our deepest fear is not that we are inadequate.
Our deepest fear is that we are powerful beyond
measure. It is our light, not our darkness, that
most frightens us. We ask ourselves, who am I
to be brilliant, gorgeous, talented and fabulous?
Actually, who are you not to be? You are a child of
God. Your playing small does not serve the world.
There is nothing enlightened about shrinking so
that other people won't feel insecure about you.
We are all meant to shine, as children do. We were
born to manifest the glory of God that is within
us. It's not just in some of us; it's in everyone. And

as we let our own light shine, we unconsciously
give other people permission to do the same. As
we are liberated from our own fear, our presence
automatically liberates others.

From Marianne Williamson, *A Return to Love: Reflections on
the Principles of 'A Course in Miracles'*, HarperCollins
(New York: 1992).

Sometimes fear causes us to forsake our values and what we
believe in. It causes the light that we possess to make this world
a brighter place to be diminished. We need to let our light shine
so that others may be able to see and be inspired by it. I have
always maintained that

it is more meaningful to *see* a sermon
than *hear* one.

And one such sermon that I have seen with my own eyes was
'preached' by my cousin whom I hold dearly as a good friend,
Apollo Perelini, on the field of rugby.

Despite fear of condemnation and ridicule from his peers
and the like, Apollo is a man prepared to live out his faith. The
event I am about to describe happened when I was playing for
Wigan against Apollo's team, St Helens. There was much rivalry
between our respective sides as we were situated in close prox-
imity to each other in the North of England. Consequently, the
tension was always at knife's edge when our two teams met.

During one such encounter, I sustained a tackle that injured
my knee quite badly. The analysis of our team physio was that

I needed to be stretchered off and that was the end of that match for me. What amazed everyone was that one of the opposition players took an end of the stretcher to carry me off. It was Apollo! Through that simple show of solidarity and overcoming the fear of 'what others may think' Apollo was also able to demonstrate to all who witnessed it that there was something much bigger at work here than the game – our faith and close friendship. Like me, Apollo always dedicated his performances on the field to God, but that moment touched everybody present as they witnessed the practical side to our shared belief.

Apollo Perelini
Currently coaching at a Dubai rugby academy
'Everything in life is about commitment.'

'When Inga talks about overcoming fear, I believe that we can learn from him because I have seen the evidence of his lack of fear on many occasions. I have known Inga pretty much all his life, from when we were seven or eight years old, way back in Kelston Primary School, then on to intermediate and high school. Eroni Clarke and Michael Jones also grew up in the same area.

'The Inga I know is not afraid of anything. I can remember when we used to walk home from our training sessions at ten or eleven at night, Inga would find it no problem to take the short cut home – through the local cemetery! As for the rest of the boys, you guessed it – we took the long way home. Inga was also someone always prepared to take a chance, to try something new, and even the thought of failing has never put him off. No one can put his flame out and he has proved many of his critics wrong on a number of occasions.

'Take, for example, his switch from union to league. Despite the critics, he went ahead. What that did for me was give me the faith to do the same. Even though league was a much different game, I had the confidence to make the switch because I saw that Inga had already done so. I was encouraged by his example to see that if it worked, then good; if not, move on. Inga's code switch and his move to England inspired a lot of Pacific Island players to consider his actions and do the same.

'After I married Selina, we also moved to England in 1994 where I took up a league contract with St Helens. Later, I switched back to union for Sale Sharks and retired in 2002, thereafter taking up coaching in 2003. Inga and Daphne were a tower of strength for us in those early days and they made a massive difference in helping us adjust to life over there as we found our feet. Inga hadn't lost his cultural identity as he always had an open-door policy at his house and you were always welcome.

'Moving away from our homeland, we experienced similar hardships to Inga and Daphne. When you are living away from your home it does help you grow, but you only realise this afterwards. For us Pacific Islanders who are used to having a closely knit family always around, initially it was a shock to be on our own away from them. I guess that's why we called around Inga's place so often, because at the time they were the only family we knew. This was something that we were able to share with our English friends as well. Hospitality is a Christian virtue that we practised. They were able to see that, with us, you didn't have to ring to visit but you could just turn up. Some may consider this inappropriate, but for us Islanders it's the norm.

'When Inga and I get together we often reflect on where we have come from to where God has taken us. We both agree that we worked hard for what we got and always say that there were more talented kids than us but the difference was we were more dedicated than them. We put in the hard yards and trained harder. I also remember how we used to train with Don Oliver at 5.30 a.m., running and training with him when we could have been at home sleeping. We had determined from an early age that we wanted to do well so we could give back to our families. We didn't come from wealthy backgrounds but we knew that you could not achieve these things without hard work. Everything in life is about commitment.

'Inga set the benchmark for where I wanted to be, and I chased after him. If Inga did it, then I was motivated to emulate him. He was the role model for us to follow in what he achieved. He was the pioneer who paved the way. In hindsight, I can confidently say that not only did Inga's move to England give me the courage to do so, it also opened doors for many other Pacific Island players who were afraid of making the switch of codes and moving to Europe. For some, the cultural differences would have been a deterrent, but having someone like Inga there would have been a confidence boost. He showed us that you could achieve what you want if you put your mind to it and never give up. Even with the All Blacks he was the first full Samoan to play for them. This hugely inspired many others to aspire to do the same.

'The great thing about Inga is that he has tempered his fame and fortune with humility and has never changed for anything. That could be a cultural thing, as some may say our culture keeps us on the ground and doesn't allow us to be big-headed. In front of other people you may be a superstar, but when you are at home you are just one of the boys. Inga and I have earned the right to speak into each other's lives and as good friends keep each other in check. We always have a laugh when we are together. Even if we have not seen each other for a long time, we always pick up from when we last met. Having Inga as a friend was, and is, priceless. He is the one person who will always be there for you, never mind the time. There is a proverb that describes my thoughts well when it says "a friend sticks closer to you than a brother". That's how Inga and I are.'

FROM ME TO YOU ABOUT INGA

- Inga always makes time for people, regardless of what he is doing.

- Inga will make the effort to put someone at ease and make them feel special, even if he has just met them for the first time.

- Inga has a genuine love and concern for others as well as great people skills.

- Inga is dedicated and committed, putting into action and following through with what he says.

- Inga is a straight talker. He never beats around the bush and is straightforward.

- Inga is never ashamed of his faith.

'I believe that whatever Inga sets out to do, he will succeed at it. Why? Because he will always put his heart and soul into it. He gives 100 per cent and never gives up – that's Inga. Anything he puts his hand to will prosper and I wish him the very best in all his endeavours.'

My cousin Apollo has learnt the lesson that to conquer the illusion of fear, you must step out in faith. I truly believe that when you are able to overcome your fear you will be liberated to perform so much better. Fear acts as an inhibitor to all that we can become. In my time playing for the All Blacks I learnt a very important truth about fear:

the fear of losing shall never override
the privilege to express one's talents.

4.

Testing and Shaping at Wigan

It's not the size of the dog in the fight,
it's the size of the fight in the dog.

Mark Twain

That first physical training session at Wigan is vivid in my memory. It was held on the top field and the conditions were a typical English winter's day: cold and wet. The coaching staff wanted to put me to the test. They wanted to find out where I was at with regard to my fitness and physical strength.

There were many lessons to be learned in my transition from union to league and no one gave me a rulebook so I could familiarise myself with the laws. I admit it could have been easier, but then I don't think it would have been as much fun. Having played in union as a winger, it was an obvious choice that they put me out on the wing – the reasoning being that it would be easier for me to learn the new game from a distance. One of my first lessons in league was in the art of 'scrambling'. Those familiar with the code will know all about it. Usually it happens when the opposition kicks the ball on their fifth tackle.

The winger's role is to pick up the ball in the first and second tackles and run on from dummy-half.

Picking up the ball in that first training session, I made my run. Surveying my options – or rather my 'victims' – my trained rugby eye was quick to pick out a puny-looking Englishman who seemed an 'easy target'. I could bowl this guy over effortlessly. Boy, was I in for a surprise! I got sat on my backside big time. The shudder that went through my whole body when he hit me was immense. I'd never felt that kind of pain from a 'white boy' tackling me before.

I wish I could say that that was the end of it, but it wasn't. I had another crack at him during that training session. This time I would surely prove that his earlier tackle was a fluke. This time I'd make certain *he* was the one that went down. Boy, was I wrong again! He sat me on my backside for the second time and totally smashed me. I couldn't believe that one of the smallest guys on the park had flattened me twice in the one training session. So much for getting off to a flying start at Wigan and making an immediate good impression! This was totally embarrassing. How could it be?

Back at the showers afterwards the mystery of why it felt like I'd just been run over by a bus was explained. This puny white boy took off his shirt to reveal his 'muscle monkeys'. He may have looked scrawny but he was ripped and his body was as hard as an ox – I knew all about that as I'd just felt the full brunt of it, not once but twice. Looks were indeed deceiving in this new game. The guy in question who had flipped me on my back turned out to be none other than the great scrum-half Shaun Edwards, captain of Great Britain and Wigan. Boy, did

I single out the wrong guy to go up against in training!

It was a rude awakening. The build of these league blokes, with their well-proportioned and battle-hardened bodies, was incredible. The long hours they put into working out at the gym, training with weights every day, made them as tough as nails. It really woke me up to the reality that I had to get my body into much better physical shape. Those early months were an absolute shocker for me. I turned up not as fit as I thought I was and should have been. By playing union at the highest level I mistakenly thought I'd done enough to make the league grade. The truth was that it took a good half-year to get myself into some respectable sort of shape to compete effectively.

In my first week I had to undertake some fitness testing. I really wanted to impress my British team-mates and the fellow Kiwi contingent that was there – Frano Botica, Dean Bell and Sam Panapa. To be brutally honest, I was an absolute disgrace. I couldn't even bench-press 115 kg properly. As for doing a proper chin-up, all I could manage was one. What made it even more humiliating was that we had the youth academy training with us. They were talented school kids of about sixteen years of age and even they were beating me week in and week out.

It also took me a little while to get my head around the whole 'professional' aspect to playing sport. You were paid to play *and* train. Initially the regime came as a complete shock: regimented training sessions and programmes to follow that started early in the morning. You were told what time you had to turn up and what you had to do. We trained twice a day, early mornings and afternoons. We got to go back home in between and come back later in the afternoon which was good as I got to pick up my kids from school and spend time with them.

Back in New Zealand you went to work and trained only twice a week, Tuesdays and Thursdays, and then played on Saturdays. The current routine was vigorous. On top of training every day and playing once a week, on the day before the game there was the 'captain's run' (when the team captain takes the team for a workout). It was not as intense but you had a good burst.

The hard, cold reality was that my unfitness exposed to me where I needed to be and it opened my eyes to the need to step up to the mark. League was certainly a very different kettle of fish to union. For a start, the game was much faster – in fact, I was blown away by just how fast it was. It was like playing a union test week in and week out. We played in so many competitions that it was not uncommon to take the field up to three times a week when the season heated up.

My body had to get accustomed to the pain that I was constantly subjecting it to as part of the relentless training and game time. It was really, really tough and that's no understatement. There were occasions when I ran so hard that I blanked out. But even the prop forwards were still beating me left, right and centre. It used to amaze me that they could run all day, and still make on average twelve tackles each time they went out on the park.

Some people might think me crazy to have continued to subject myself to this level of discomfort. But that was all part and parcel of the wonderful challenge I had in front of me. Sure, I could have felt sorry for myself, packed my bags and hopped on the next plane back to New Zealand with my tail between my legs. What inspired me to stick with it was the collective effort that I saw in evidence at Wigan. This truly great team was renowned for decades of outstanding achievements. That shared will to win was their hallmark. Just like the All Blacks, the priority was not the individual – whoever put on the team jersey was focused not on themselves but the team.

However, it is one thing to be a part of a team but quite another thing to contribute to it as well. A team full of champions is no promise of a champion team. In most sports you always have your prima donnas. At Wigan, individuals had to learn to let go of their egos for the team to succeed.

One is too small a number to achieve greatness
(John Maxwell).

These guys lived and breathed that ethos. And here I was playing alongside the likes of Martin 'Chariots' Offiah, Shaun Edwards, Sam Panapa, Dean Bell. These players were bona fide 'living legends' of the game, and I was out there in the middle with them.

When I arrived at Wigan, the season, which started in August and went through till about May, was already well under way. The good news was that the more I trained the fitter and stronger and more confident I became, and the more I started to enjoy my game. I played my first match about six or seven weeks after arrival. What a delight it was to score on debut, right on 80 minutes, against Widnes. Former Wigan chairman Jack Robinson was one of those taking a keen interest in the progress of their new 'convert'.

Jack Robinson

Former Wigan Warriors chairman

'Inga proved that just because you're a Christian, doesn't mean you can't dish it out on the field . . .'

'There was no doubt in my mind when I saw Inga play union that he was a fantastic player. A real game-breaker and someone who I believed at the time was the best union backline player in the world. My first reaction on watching one of Inga's games for the All Blacks was 'wow'. I was totally impressed by his power, speed, guile and ability to step for such a big man. My mind immediately went to imagining him as a league player and seeing how devastating he could be in our Wigan backline. Being such a worldwide name in rugby union, I knew it would be very hard to get someone like him to sign for us. Nevertheless, we threw our hat in the ring and expressed our desire to sign him. Inga's agent arranged for us to meet and the rest, as they say, is history.

'From the feedback I used to receive from our conditioning coach, Chris Butler, I believe that Inga was not in the best of shape to begin with. We had a job on our hands getting him up to speed, and all credit to Inga as he stuck in there and never quit. His commitment showed when he was changed physically and conditioned into a well-proportioned powerhouse of a league player – or in the words of some of the sports commentators, a 'man mountain'. What was amazing was that Inga had maintained his starting weight but had gained a lot of muscle mass and shed a few inches around the sides. He was truly a fearful opponent for any opposition.

'It's no secret that initially Inga had to fight his way into the team. We already had two acclaimed wingers in Martin Offiah and the young up-and-coming Jason Robinson. But it wasn't long before Inga made his debut and what a reward it was for us when he scored right on the 80th minute. To accommodate his playing ability and for the good of the team, Inga was slotted into centre. He was a very special player playing in a backline I considered the best that union or league could offer at the time. You had the exhilarating Jason Robinson who mesmerised the opposition by stepping both ways, our leading try-scorer and thunderbolt, Martin Offiah, the reliable and solid Gary Connolly, and alongside him lined up Inga who turned out to be the best centre we ever signed. The scoring power of that backline was testament to their calibre – just ask any of our opponents of the time about how they felt taking the park against us.

'With Inga on the field, something special was always sure to happen. He had the ability to beat the man and possessed a more brilliant pair of hands than just about any backline player I have ever seen. Add to this his fantastic passing ability, which was evidenced when he would have about three men tackling him but he would still be able to get the ball away. His defensive play was equally remarkable – there wasn't anything you could say against his game. Forever etched in my mind is a try Inga scored against the world's best at the time, the touring Australian national team. It was an absolutely brilliant try and it was scored against another great player, Mal Meninga. There was much hype about Inga versus Mal, and I can remember Inga chipping over him, stooping and picking up the ball and then having to beat another player and then the fullback as well. Against the best in the world, Inga came out tops.

'Wigan scored both on and off the field with signing Inga. The fans, players and management alike warmed to him and his personality. He was a good man for the club who always supported his team-mates. We had some rough players at the time, and I believe that Inga was able to have a positive effect on some of those lads. He was always prepared to give his time and was someone the young academy lads could look up to. He used to spend time with them and give them advice to help them along their way. Some might say that if Inga was so good for Wigan, then why did we allow him to leave and not do more to keep him? As much as I wanted to keep Inga, I knew that he had given his all for Wigan. One thing I learnt as chairman of the club is that if someone's heart is elsewhere and if they have given their best for you, then it's up to you to do the best for them. Inga Tuigamala was a very straight and honourable man and I owed it to him to be the same. His move to Newcastle was another stage in his life and I applaud him for being bold enough to return to union. While Inga was a player that every Wiganer was proud to have in their team, he was also much sought after and we knew we couldn't hold on to him any longer.'

FROM ME TO YOU ABOUT INGA

- Inga is a man of impeccable integrity and so was the obvious choice at a time when I needed a character witness for myself.

- Inga is a genuine all-round person who will never let you down – any parent would be proud to have a son like him.

- Inga is able to stand his ground and yet still maintain his faith – he proved that just because you're a Christian, doesn't mean you can't dish it out on the field, yet always within the rules and with a sincere handshake after the game.

- Inga is the man I would choose if I was ever in the trenches and had a choice of just one man to be there with me, for sure.

As you can see, the big challenge of those early days was to step up to the mark – do or die, I had to enter the furnace and come out the other end, refined. There was no other way.

5.

Keep Stepping Up, Never Down

It is a rough road that leads
to the heights of greatness.

Seneca

B y experiencing its initial demands, I understood what was meant by the comment 'playing league requires a different type of athlete altogether from union'. In union – at least as it was played back then – there was plenty of time to catch your breath at a lineout, scrum or restart, but in league you didn't have the luxury of time as it was all go right from the whistle. There were not many stoppages and as a result it required a fitness level beyond what I was accustomed to in the other code. This did not dampen my spirits at all but rather made me more determined to step up to the mark and not give up without a fight. We all have to accept that life is always going to be full of challenges – the key to overcoming them is to keep pressing on. You've got to take the good with the bad and roll with the punches.

At the outset of this book I mentioned that you could expect honesty from me. This is why I have revealed the naked truth about my shortcomings in fitness when I arrived at Wigan – to drive home the point that we will all go through times in our life when we need to overcome rather than be overcome. The following story is a good object lesson on overcoming these periods of adversity:

A farmer's donkey fell down into a well and cried piteously for hours. Finally, the farmer decided the animal was old and the well needed to be covered up anyway; it just wasn't worth it trying to retrieve the donkey. He invited all his neighbours to come over and help him shovel dirt into the well. At first, the donkey realised what was happening and cried horribly. Then, he quietened down. Curious, the farmer peered down the well and was astonished. With every shovel of dirt that hit its back, the donkey was doing something amazing. He would shake it off and take a step up. As the farmer's neighbours continued to shovel dirt on top of the animal, he kept shaking it off and taking another step up. Pretty soon, everyone was amazed as the donkey stepped up over the edge of the well and trotted off!

Plainly, the moral of the story is that sooner or later we too will find ourselves in situations where the 'dirt' is getting shovelled on us; situations when we feel as though we're getting buried under by the pressures of this world. Allowing ourselves to get caught up in self-pity and negativity will only keep us down in the pit longer. Like that donkey, once we've stopped the crying and focused on finding a way out, what we need to do is take what is being used to bury us and build a platform with it to step up out of the mess. I strongly believe that the tests and obstacles that we encounter in our lives come our way to strengthen us if we choose to face them. Each trial can be a stepping stone to success if we never give up; if we *shake off the dirt and take a step up*!

People admire and strive to emulate their sports idols, but are they prepared to pay the same price? There's always a cost factor involved in anyone achieving their dreams. You certainly can't sit on your behind and expect things to happen for you. You have to be prepared to go out and make it happen. The trouble is that we don't want to be confronted with change and problems. We want the glamour and all the trappings that come along with success but are not prepared to make the necessary sacrifices. This is why it saddens me when I look around and see that we live in a world that is so imbued with the ethos of comfort. Anything that is seen as making us uncomfortable is shunned. This creates the false impression that life is all about us being comfortable. Take it from me, in order to achieve success in life you will be required to step out of your comfort zone. No two ways about it, you must be prepared to put in the hard yards and do the necessary work. If being comfortable in life is all you are aiming for, then you will miss out on so much more that you could achieve.

I knew that for me to excel at Wigan I had to be prepared to stretch myself. I couldn't do it in the game as that wasn't the place for it. Where could I do it? At the training! Playing the game was the easy part. It was the training that took a lot out of you. That's the place where you would stretch and grow. You couldn't expect to 'turn it on' come game day if you hadn't put in the hard yards at training. So my goal became to give my all in the training sessions and not hold back – and in the famous words of champion golfer Gary Player,

'the harder you practise, the luckier you get'.

Some folks like to believe that there's some kind of mystique to sporting success. Believe you me, there are no secrets to success. No magic formulas. It just comes down to hard work. Or as I like to say:

success isn't *hocus pocus*
but all about *being focused.*

Somebody I've admired greatly in life and who taught me much about training is the former New Zealand champion weightlifter, the late great Don Oliver. During the time we spent together over the years we developed a close relationship that extended far beyond the gym. Don truly inspired me and through his example emphasised to me the truth that when you take the time to put in the effort to train and be committed to it then the results will come. One particular saying that he used often inspired me and holds true in so many aspects of life:

'Train with dedication and play with expectation.'

Let me pay tribute to Don by sharing with you the impact he had upon me and many, many others.

Don Oliver
Trainer, mentor, and man ahead of his time
'Strong back, strong man – weak back, weak man . . .'

Don Oliver had a real passion for promoting health and well-being. He was instrumental in coaching not just me but also former All Blacks and close friends of mine Eroni Clarke and Michael Jones at his gym in West Auckland. Rugby was still amateur in those days, so when we weren't training with the All Black or Auckland teams, we'd head down to Don's gym. As a champion sportsman in his specialised field of weightlifting, Don taught us a lot about the proper and effective use of weights in our training sessions.

Don believed that we needed to warm our body temperature up before we got into the stretching and full-on training sessions. So he'd get us to sit in the sauna beforehand. On some of those occasions he used to come and join us clad in tracksuit and hat. To inspire us, he'd quote verses from the Bible. What amazed Michael Jones and me, though, was not so much his biblical knowledge, but that for those 10 to 12 minutes we were in the sauna, he *never* broke into a sweat!

Don's famous admonishment to us was

'Strong back, strong man – weak back, weak man'.

He always emphasised this principle to us in our training and got us to focus on strengthening our lower backs and stomach areas – the region of the body now commonly known as the 'core'. But Don was drilling this into us way back in the late eighties and early nineties, whereas the fitness industry has only begun promoting this 'core' aspect to our health and well-being relatively recently. This and many other aspects of Don's training regimen confirm that he was truly a man ahead of his time.

I will always remember Don as a man who had a genuine rapport with other people and a committed faith in God. His love for others oozed out of him so naturally. He always had a laugh to share and wore an infectious smile from ear to ear. The valuable life lesson I learnt from being around him is that with all the cares of living, sometimes we neglect the pleasure of simply spending time with each other. No matter how busy he was, Don always made time for you. Whenever you were in his presence, he made you feel special.

Not surprisingly, Don was a man of few words who let his actions do the talking. He taught us to stand tall and be proud of ourselves regardless of our race or faith. Even down to his last breath, I was told that he was still inspiring the nurses and doctors who tended to him. I was overseas at the time of his passing on and therefore could not be at his funeral. Maureen can be so proud that she was the wife to this wonderful man who saw no limits and instilled in us all such important life values. As a young man growing up I couldn't help but look to Don as a role model on how I was to conduct myself.

As a sportsman constantly in the limelight, the focus was always on what I achieved on the playing field. By now you will have realised that that was the easy part. My advice is that if you are serious about your sport then it starts by being serious about your training for it.

> Before you can *play* as a champion,
> you have to learn to *train* as one first.

I know this because as a professional athlete I was programmed to train up to six days a week and then to let it all out in that 80 minutes of match time. There's no other way to achieve your dreams of playing in the big time. Like many Kiwi boys, my dream was to play rugby for the All Blacks. I thank God for the athletic gift that he gave me but I knew that wasn't going to be enough in itself to turn my dream into a reality. We are all born with talent and ability – it's what we choose to do with it that counts.

The choices I've made have left me with no regrets. Those choices allowed me to achieve the success that I have enjoyed thus far. I can remember times when my friends would come around to entice me to accompany them out partying and boozing. I chose not to. I was absolutely dedicated to my dream and determined to give myself every chance in my power to make it come true. However, if you believe that I acquired this resilience and never-say-die attitude solely from my playing days, you would be wrong. I also owe a lot to the example set by my parents.

Life wasn't always easy for me growing up. I was by no means born with a silver spoon in my mouth. When we immigrated to New Zealand from Samoa, we had to adapt to new surroundings in a foreign country. To make matters more difficult, as you will have read, my father died when I was young. Mum was left to bring up her fourteen children by herself. Did she pack it all in and give up? No, she didn't. Fuelled by her love for us, it was her tenacity that held us together as a family. This is one of the reasons why I place such a premium on the importance of family. When the going got tough, we stuck together and we all pulled through.

Similarly, I encourage others to persevere through the tough times. Even though it seemed as though life had offered me less opportunity, I was able to turn that less around to achieve so much more. And whilst there were many occasions on which I could have felt sorry for myself, I chose not to indulge in self-pity. My mum's example is to persevere through the tough times, and it's an example I want to instil in my kids and the people I meet – including anyone reading this book – as well.

Not quitting when things got tough is the character-building principle that has stood me in good stead all through my life. This is why I can confidently say that giving up in my early days at Wigan was never going to be an option – although I'd be lying if I said that it didn't cross my mind once or twice. But here we were in England, and I wasn't going to give up without a fight – without giving my best! Like basketball legend Michael Jordan,

> I can accept failure; everyone fails at something.
> But I can't accept not even trying.

In my first six months at Wigan when my body was adjusting to the new demands of league, I remember many a time returning from the training sessions bruised and battered. In the early hours of the morning Daphne used to run the bath so that I could ease my aching body. Looking back, I can see the funny side, because I was like another child to be attended to, but believe you me the soreness that I was experiencing was no laughing matter at the time! Seeing me in so much pain she used to ask the hard question, 'Why don't we just go back to New Zealand if you're finding it so hard here?' But was that the more rewarding option?

Well, was it worth it? Experiencing all that pain and discomfort? You bet ya! Opportunities don't get handed to you on a silver platter in this life. Rest assured, there will be an element of pain associated with anything worthwhile. As they say, 'no pain, no gain'. Let me conclude this chapter with the motivational words of the heavyweight boxing great Muhammad Ali, who said:

> 'Nothing is impossible. I hate every minute
> of training. But I say don't quit. Suffer now
> and live the rest of your life as a champion.'

My time at Wigan

Season	Appearances	Tries	Goals	Points
1993–94	11	4	–	16
1994–95	39	25	–	100
1995–96	26	20	–	80
1996–97	26	13	3	58
TOTAL	102	62	3	254

6.

Influence

Setting an example is not the main means
of influencing another, it is the only means.

Albert Einstein

To succeed in life you have to be at the forefront setting the pace. That's the advice his mum gave to my good friend Michael Jones. She went on to say that you should never be the tail as it is always better to be the head. So my outlook in life is that I want to be at the forefront of what happens and not following blindly what others are doing. I am a strong believer in not accepting the status quo.

This is an area where I believe so many young people are getting into trouble. You don't have to follow what others are doing to feel accepted or have a sense of belonging. You have a responsibility to give yourself every opportunity to succeed in life. You owe it to yourself to be your biggest asset and not your worst liability. I urge you to be an asset to yourself. How, you may ask? By making wise choices as to how you live your life. What may feel right because others are doing it may not necessarily be the right choice. In my life I have been tempted to get into drugs, alcohol and live a lifestyle that could have destroyed all that I had built. I chose not to, and that's a choice that you have before you as well. It may require you to make some hard choices as to who you choose to hang around with.

The company of the friends that we keep can be a big influence on our lives. I experienced that truth first-hand when I used to belong to a gang in my early teens. At the time, it was the cool thing to do. I got the shock of my life when one of my best friends got stabbed with a screwdriver during a brawl with a rival gang. Thankfully, he didn't die, but that incident gave me a real jolt and brought home to me the reality of how dangerous that lifestyle was. It could have been me. It made me sit up and really assess my future. In the thoughtful words of the Bible proverb:

'There is a way that seems right to a man,
but in the end it leads to destruction.'

I didn't want to be another youth statistic and I was glad to leave that meaningless lifestyle behind and grateful that my interest and talent in rugby allowed me to pursue another avenue.

Another good example of what I am talking about is my very good friend, former team-mate at Wigan and former England captain, Jason Robinson. When I first met Jason he was about twenty years old. He was an up-and-coming star. From the talent he possessed it was clearly evident that he was destined for greater things. Jason had the ability to beat players left, right and centre. He was blessed with the ability to give defenders nightmares as he could step both sides off either of his feet. Even before Jason set foot on the rugby field, I was in awe of what he was capable of at training. He could do things that I thought were beyond the ability of a normal human being. And whatever he did, he did at a hundred miles an hour. Whether it was training or playing, he put his everything into it. That's how he got the apt nickname 'Billy Whizz' after a character in the British comic *Beano* who is extremely fast.

There would have been plenty of reasons for anyone coming from Jason Robinson's difficult background to have gone off the rails of life and stayed there. Raised in a single-parent home from birth, and later experiencing the horror of living in an environment dominated by domestic violence, his life is a testimony in itself to triumph over adversity. His tremendous resilience and rugby-playing talent was the reprieve that enabled him to become who he is today. But with the success, as Jason will tell you, came another series of challenges which could well have ruined him. Jason made a decision to change and it was one that I believe is the greatest decision anyone will have to make.

Through rugby, Jason had money and would get more money; but the more he got, the more he realised that it wasn't providing him true fulfilment. He admits that he used to try to find this fulfilment in alcohol, chasing after women, or indulging his passion for fancy cars. Meanwhile, he was playing his best rugby, and receiving plenty of pats on the back for the great things he was doing on the sports field. Away from that, he admits that he was miserable, alone, empty and the total opposite to what everyone thought they saw when they looked at him on the field. A warrant out for his arrest for failing to appear in court on an assault charge, and generally struggling to cope with the responsibilities of life – he was in a right mess. Jason fully accepts that he was in the wrong place at the wrong time, but it was largely due to the lifestyle that he was choosing to live.

Through the friendship we shared both on and off the pitch, I managed to have an influence on Jason's life when we were together at Wigan. So much so that Jason mentioned it in his book, *Finding My Feet*, written after his triumph as part of the England rugby team in winning the 2003 IRB Rugby World Cup. I invited him to share his thoughts about our friendship and the influence it has had on his life.

Jason Robinson
Dual league and union international
'Inga was a man that made a massive impact in more ways than one.'

'Inga was known by a lot of different names when he first arrived at Wigan – before people managed to learn how to correctly pronounce his name ("Twingimala" and "Tugimala" were a couple of the more popular ones in the early days). In the locals' defence, not many Samoans had ventured to the North of England at that time, so they didn't have much practice. However, it didn't take them long to get the hang of it as very soon he was the talk of the town. Such is the legacy of Va'aiga Tuigamala that even today, some thirteen years after his departure, you'll still hear people singing his praises there. Inga was a man that made a massive impact in more ways than one.

'However, all that we knew at the time was that we had signed an All Black. Now, that didn't mean too much to us as league was the game that was mostly played in the North of England, and anything union was frowned upon. Wigan was the most successful league club in the world at the time. We already had a very good team and, to be honest, signing Inga didn't mean that much to us. We knew that he was a big name but we didn't realise how big. What's more, we were told that he was a church-goer – something that, outside of attending wedding, funeral or baptism services, it's probably fair to say was a foreign concept to the vast majority of the club membership.

'Enter Va'aiga Tuigamala. My first impression was that he was not that tall (look who's talking: I'm only five foot eight), but he was clearly a big strong bloke. Martin Offiah and I held the two winger spots in the side, so I was a bit nervous that my regular place on the team could be threatened – you know what they say, "two's company but three's a crowd". I really couldn't see the need for signing another winger.

'When Inga arrived his fitness was nowhere near our level. To be honest, I couldn't see why the club had forked out so much for him. I came in to this level in 1992 as a seventeen-year-old, trained twice a day and ate, drank and slept league.

But all credit to Inga as he stuck to his guns and didn't give up. Over time he got into real great shape and was ever-menacing on the field. In fact, he soon became one of those players you hoped you wouldn't run into on the field – I was so glad he was on *my* team. But in those early days, what Inga lacked in fitness he more than made up for with his formidable ball skills. I remember many of the lads agreeing that for a big man he was extremely skilful.

'All the same, I was very sceptical of anyone that openly professed their faith in God. Making a widely known decla-ration that he was a Christian soon made him a target on the field by the opposition. As a Christian, people automatic-ally thought that he was going to be soft, but he was hard and played within the laws, and tough, if not tougher than anyone else. Also, when you make the code switch the op-position want to 'welcome' you to the league with some hard hits and tackles. They thought they could knock him about, but it was the other way around most of the time. Even when he was getting pushed around on the park he didn't retaliate though.

'I remember thinking that he seemed to be the happiest person at the club and I couldn't understand why. We would always be out drinking and turning up the following morning with our breaths stinking of alcohol. To take the mickey out of him, some of the lads used to breathe on him deliberately. (They didn't need to breathe on him for him to get the smell, as it was powerful enough to be picked up from at least five metres away!) All Inga would do was have a laugh and never condemn them or get agitated. At least, he never showed it if he did, and just carried on his merry way.

'A pivotal moment and one that could have caused our friendship to take a turn for the worse happened at the time of the 1994 Challenge Cup final against Leeds when I was dropped in favour of Inga. I was furious and couldn't believe I'd been dropped. The coach at the time, John Dorahy, assured me that if I played in the reserve team and produced the goods he would consider me for the final. I did and scored three tries. When he announced the team for the final I was even more upset as Inga was in and I was out. Inga had taken my winger spot. What Inga did after the squad was announced I believe was a defining moment for our friendship. I can remember him just damping out the flames straight away by coming over to comfort me for not making the final. I don't remember exactly what he said, but I do know it just cleared the air. In the spirit of professionalism, it should have been me going to him and offering congratulations. He probably realised that I was a bit immature. Even though I was furious at the time, by his actions he made it so that my heart was not poisoned towards him and I greatly respect him for doing that.

'I know it may seem selfish on my part, but I maintain that Inga came to Wigan in 1994 just for me. I was drinking quite heavily, frequenting nightclubs and fooling around with girls. I had given in to the pressures of being in the limelight with all the fame and fortune of being a professional sportsman. At the time, I did what I did to prove that I was one of the boys.

Inga didn't buy into any of that rubbish. In the treatment room he would sit there and read away contentedly with his Bible. Although he was no Bible-basher, at the same time he didn't attempt to hide his life. In those days I was against Christianity, but even I had to acknowledge that there was something different about him.

'I've seen some real hard rugby players – the sort you'd normally be intimidated by – really transforming in his presence, even to the point of going out of their way to apologise to him for swearing. Before one of our finals the local paper asked one of my drinking partners who was the character in the team, the prop Neil Cowie, to do a slapstick profile on our team members before the game. He took the mick out of all of us using the following sort of language – 'big, fat, ugly, can't get a girlfriend' – and we got ripped. However, for Inga there was a lot of respect and he described him something like this: "Va'aiga Tuigamala – born-again Christian who never gets cross." That was testament to the respect that the fellows had for Inga.

'I looked at the family life that Inga had and I wanted something like that for myself. People were always welcome at his house. When I used to visit I'd ask him who somebody was and he would reply it was his cousin. I remember thinking that he must have had a few million cousins! That was the Inga that I knew – always inviting people to come around to his place and showing hospitality. They were like a Pacific Island tribe that had started to colonise the north of

England with their culture of hospitality and caring. I confess that I had never seen the likes of this before I met Inga.'

THE DREAM

'I remember the fateful day when Inga came up to me and asked if he could share a dream he'd had about me. In his dream he'd seen me standing on top of the world with the world under my feet. As he watched, the world started to crumble beneath me. How had he known how messed up his twenty-year-old team-mate's life was? Through his dream he really touched on the fact that something was lacking in my life. It really hurt that I had no father to turn to, having never known him. The only people I had were the guys – and if you go to rugby players and say you have a problem, their typical response is to say, "Let's go have a pint." In their way they're trying to help you, but it only makes things worse. What Inga said to me was like an arrow that pierced my heart.

'At the time, I was with a girl with whom I had a baby out of marriage and had just got news that I had made another girl pregnant. Because of this I was drinking even more to drown my problems. Just as in Inga's dream, the world was disintegrating beneath me. I needed to take better control of my life:

only dead fish go with the flow.

He invited me to come along and sit down with a few of his friends for a Bible study that they called "Just Looking". I could handle that. Apollo Perelini was also there. So with him and Inga beside me I felt at ease because I had a lot of respect for them for their exploits on-field. I can remember Frano Botica, Shaun Edwards and Henry Paul joining in too.

'Those Bible studies made me question lots of things that were happening in my life. Because of the background I was coming from I thought that if I had "x, y, z" then all would be solved. The God of the Bible showed me that without him I had absolutely nothing. In order to change, I needed to ask the Lord into my life. That year I did, and it's because of the example he set that I believe Inga was sent to Wigan for me in 1994. Forget the rugby. I'm not saying he's perfect either. What I saw was a godly man who had the conviction to live out his faith and not be diverted by the temporal attractions of this world. After I made the decision to follow Jesus it became even more of a pleasure to play alongside Inga and our friendship became even stronger. We were brothers – his million cousins were now my cousins. Like a little brother, I wanted to imitate him, and because he used to put a cross on his wrist I also started doing that to show people that I too was a Christian. People like to blame their environment for their problems, but I have learnt to put God first and try to live the right life within my calling, which has now led me into the realm of coaching. For this and countless other blessings, I will always be thankful that Inga shared his dream with me.'

FROM ME TO YOU ABOUT INGA

- Inga is a godly man; a man who walks the talk and backs up words with action.

- Inga is a man of integrity and morals, yet he enjoys life and isn't serious all the time.

- Inga, the ex-All Black and league star who switched codes and reached great heights in each game, has been a tremendous role model not just for me but for everyone he has come in contact with, and it is my hope that this book gives people an insight into the person behind those on-field achievements.

'After a few years when he had left Wigan and went to play for Newcastle, I played against Inga in union as I had switched to Sale Sharks. I remember going round to have dinner at his house the night before we played – not something you normally do with the opposition on the eve of a game. Even though he was coming to the back end of his career and didn't quite have his former speed, his mind was still as sharp as ever. Our wingers knew that if they got the opportunity they could get around him, but if they were waiting for the ball they could expect to get blindsided by him. Every opportunity he got to fly out and smash a fellow he used to make them pay. It was a sight that was always good to see as long as it wasn't you getting smashed! Thankfully, our paths didn't cross that day.

'Even though I don't speak to Inga that often, I am still trying to live out the influence he has left upon me. If I can have the same effect on others as he had on me, even in a small way, I will be happy. Now, as I start a new era in my life as the head coach for Sale Sharks, I draw strength from our experiences together all those years ago. I hope that as you read this book you will get to know the real Inga, not just what you may have seen on TV, and learn more about who he is and what makes him tick. I believe that he still has a lot more to offer and eagerly wait to hear and see what God still has in store for this blessed man.'

As Jason Robinson so rightly says, 'dead fish go with the flow'. Don't be someone who is easily led astray. Be somebody who makes wise choices to live out their dreams and to continue to live them out. Jason was living out his dream of playing professional rugby, but had he continued with the lifestyle he'd adopted, his playing career may not have ended up on the high of winning the Rugby World Cup in 2003 and appearing in the 2007 final. His personal experience is testimony to the fact that

ability may get you to the top,
but it is *character* that keeps you there
(John Wooden).

Our lives need to be shining examples – and not so much by what we say as what we do. Jason has honestly revealed that he was watching me when I arrived at Wigan. More so when he heard that I was a Christian. He acknowledges that what drew him to me initially was not so much what I said but what he saw was happening in my life. My advice to others is that if you want to make a difference in people's lives you don't have to be hounding them all the time. Instead, follow the example of St Francis of Assisi:

preach the Gospel at all times,
and when necessary use words.

Doing my level best
for Wigan.

Newcastle Sevens team.
PAt Lam is seated fourth
from left, bottom row.

In Action for the
New Zealand
Colts, 1987.

Daphne and I
in Samoa 2007

With my friends Andrew Blowers (left) and Pat Lam.

Christmas morning
in Newcastle,
Samoan style!

My daughter, Salote.

Mum.

My Family, 2009.

With the Family prior to receiving Chief Title in Sa'anapu

Seeing Myan Subrayan off before he
leaves for England to do his interviews
for this book

Inga, David Tua and Subrayan Family.

My great friend
and mentor,
Kevin Roberts.

The kids with their grandma -
Pulelua Lealuga Tuigamala.

With my Pastor Tavale at
book launch in November 2009.

With Daphne and the boys.

My Boys with the boxing legend Sugar Ray Leonard.

Final of the Tetley
Cup at Twickenham.
My sons were ball
boys that day!

7.

Newcastle, Here We Come

You can never really live anyone else's life,
not even your child's. The influence you exert
is through your own life, and what you've
become yourself.

Eleanor Roosevelt

During Wigan's extended off-season break in 1996 I was allowed a six-month loan spell with the rugby union team Wasps, around the time union was just starting to turn professional. During my time with them I helped Wasps to a national title, the Tetley Premiership, which was the same title that I helped Newcastle lift later on.

It was through my time at Wasps that the union world took notice of me again. As always, there were plenty of other options I could have explored, such as back in New Zealand or Australia, but a wonderful opportunity to return to the code in the northern hemisphere came out of nowhere from the Newcastle Falcons. Newcastle's then Director of Rugby Rob Andrew, who was also a player, steered the whole process. The deal was worth a lot of money, and would assure sound security for me and my family. It was a big salary increase from what I was getting at Wigan and I couldn't have asked for better than that, so I signed the five-and-a-half-year contract.

Wigan totally understood that I had to seize the opportunity presented to me to venture further up north. Yes, there was some disappointment that I wouldn't be able to continue with Wigan, but in hindsight it was the right decision. I am forever grateful to them for caring for and embracing us in a way that was indescribable. Likewise, I appreciate that they were patient in my early days when my body had to adapt to the demands of the league game, but my days with Wigan had come to an end and it was time to move on. I'd like to think that I did justice and more than repaid them for the faith they showed in me during my stay there. As you will have read in the testimonial from former Wigan chairman Jack Robinson in Chapter 4, I parted with the club on good terms.

Frequently, the difference between a successful individual and one who ends up with regrets is vision – or the lack of it. Too many of us miss the opportunity to move ahead in life because we lack vision. The way I see it, vision is all about having an eye for opportunity and then going out and grabbing that opportunity with both hands. Friends of mine have procrastinated in the past and bitterly regretted it –

procrastination is the assassin of opportunity.

You have to seize your chances in life when they come along – consequently, I have no regrets about my departure from Wigan.

The move to Newcastle gave me the opportunity to be reunited with Pat Lam (present coach of the Auckland Blues

and captain of Manu Samoa when I played for them), whom
Newcastle had also signed. I guess Rob Andrew thought, 'Why
sign one Samoan when you can sign two?' At the time, Newcastle
was in the second division and Rob was keen to have me come
in to help with promotion. Not a problem.

Rob Andrew
**Former union international and England's
current Director of Elite Rugby**
*'He just ran right over the top of me and didn't even slow down
. . . It was like I wasn't even there!'*

'My first impression – or better stated – my first *encounter*
with Inga was when I played against him in the 1993 Lions
tour of New Zealand. It was in our second test against the
All Blacks in Wellington that I had the chance to learn first-
hand what a formidable force he was in rugby.

'I was on the receiving end of an All Black set play called
"Rangi One Out". Incidentally the "Rangi Play" was a
standard move that was invented by a Māori player who
used to play at centre. It was a brilliant move which
involved the first five passing to the second five and then
the centre going across the field bringing the winger into
the centre channel. I could see this whole move unfolding
in front of me and I knew that it was coming – the ball
ended up in Inga's hands and he was like a freight train
bearing down on me. He just ran right over the top of me

and didn't even slow down. Perhaps I did manage to slow him down a bit, but I was like a small road bump. It was like I wasn't even there! My only consolation was that although we lost the series 2–1, we did win the test in Wellington that day.

'The town of Newcastle was making news for signing what was then the most expensive player, Alan Shearer, for fifteen million pounds for the soccer club. It was a world record at the time. Newcastle rugby was still in the second division and club chairman Sir John Hall wanted an equivalent signing to help in the rebuilding of the team. So when he asked me who I'd like to sign if money was no objective, I said I knew just the guy. Naturally, that man was Inga.

'I knew that he'd been on loan with Wasps and they were keen to sign him back to union so I had to act fast. Inga came to my house with his agent where I explained that we saw him as a big part of our future plans: it was about building a structure and team. It took us several months to negotiate terms as it was a big contract. The way things turned out, we were able to pull off a Samoan double with the signing of Pat Lam of Manu Samoa as well. In fact, all the players came from different cultures and we had some big wins as we were a team full of internationals. Jonny Wilkinson came through as an eighteen-year-old at the time that Inga signed for us and it was truly a fantastic side that got us back into the premier league and then on to win it as well.

'Rugby is always in the shadows of soccer in Newcastle, but

1997 through to 2004 was one of the most exciting periods of the club's history. Most of the internationals we signed were like Inga, playing towards the end of their careers, and it was like they were doing missionary work for union in the North of England which was traditionally a league area. Inga was in superb physical condition when he came to Newcastle. He had the ability to lift and carry the team. When he had the ball he made defenders stop, which put a lot of his mates into space, and through his sheer presence he created more chances than what he scored. He would come flying in off the wing and make these crunching ball-and-all tackles (often wingers get it wrong and come in off their line too quick, but not Inga) that spectators in the crowd could almost feel.

'Towards the end when Inga was losing his speed we used to play him at centre. We had a set play that involved him chasing the box kick that usually Jonny would execute with precision. If we thought the opposition fullback was likely to drop the ball because he knew Inga was chasing it we'd let Inga loose. Imagine the ball is kicked high in the air and you're under it, waiting for it to descend. But this colossus of a man is bearing down on you like a herd of rhino and as soon as you catch it you're going to take the brunt of his impact. Either you catch the ball and get catapulted ten yards or you drop it. You could see the realisation going through their faces. Apart from Inga, I can't name too many players with that kind of ability to put the fear of God in you – literally!

'Inga was one of those guys that inspired people both on and off the field. Our supporters, sponsors, the kids at festivals, all used to be enthralled by his personality. He always had time for people and will be long remembered for his perpetual smile too. His trailblazing presence opened the door for other Pacific Islanders to play in England as well. Inga was great at encouraging younger players, as they looked up to him. I remember him helping Epe and Soa, a pair of Tongan teenagers who ended up living with him and also playing at Newcastle and imparting a bit of the Island way of life. Then there was the Samoan pastor he met who ended up becoming our number one supporter and unofficial chaplain of sorts.

'The Tetley Challenge Cup final game in 1998 was when he showed his true worth as a player. Almost on fulltime we won a lineout which should have gone to the opposition. The ball went wide and we scored a try that Jonny converted and we won right on the last minute. We beat Harlequins with the last play of the game to win the Cup – which meant Inga was the first player to win both cups in league and union. He played a huge role in that win which is one I'll always remember.

'Towards the end of 2001, Inga came to me asking to be released from his contract as he felt that he had given all that he could. I wanted to keep his fire alive for one more year so asked him to stay on. We were going through a transition as we had a lot of younger players and I wanted him to stick around and mentor them. You needed a senior player to ground the younger guys. Inga was that person. Even if he wasn't in the starting lineup, just by being in the change room and talking to the boys he was inspiring for the team. I didn't play him as often as I would have liked to, but I did it to help him as his body had taken a battering and it helped with the recovery and also to keep him match hungry.

'Let me finish by saying that Inga Tuigamala is a true legend of the game. His contribution to Newcastle Falcons both on and off the field for almost five years is incalculable. I hope that he and his family remember his time with us as a positive experience, because that was what we tried to create as a club – not only for the players but their families as well.'

That Tetley Cup final at Twickenham ranks as one of my most memorable games for Newcastle. No side had ever done what we had in coming up from the second division to take the premiership by storm the very next season. Rob Andrew had compiled a championship-winning team, crammed with internationals: Alan Tait and Doddie Weir from Scotland, Marius Hurter of South Africa, my good friend Pat Lam and more. When Jonny kicked the conversion in the dying seconds I remember whacking the ground on the halfway line and crying for joy. Although I didn't score a try, it was an honour to be named man of the match – we really thought we'd blown our chances but we dug in and took it out right on the wire.

When Jonny Wilkinson came to Newcastle as an eighteen-year-old Rob Andrew asked me and Pat Lam to take him under our wing. When he travelled along with us to a European match against Perpignan, Pat and I were totally amazed when we went down to see him catching the balls for Rob beforehand. When it came time for Johnny's turn to kick he slotted every shot from each side. 'I think we've got a winner here with this boy,' said Pat. 'He's definitely going places and will be a real star.' Not only was he a talented kicker but a ferocious tackler as well – in fact, he was an absolutely crazy tackler, a typical British bulldog, and could take out some big guys. Pat used to joke that he must have some Pacific Island blood in him seeing as he could put in such big hits!

I truly respect Rob Andrew's decision to step aside and hand over the first five spot to Jonny when he did – that to me was a sign of a great man when he recognised that his time was up. It was a privilege to have belonged to the club at the same time as both men – one in the closing days and the other in the early days of his professional career. Of course, Jonny went on to play for England, and the rest, as they say, is history. It was a privilege to witness such a wonderful young man developing into the world-class player he was to become.

Over time, as I lost my pace, I was increasingly finding my place in the centres where I used my strength to bowl over as many of the opposition as I could. However, towards the end of 2001 after every game I could feel that this old bull was ready to be taken out and shot. I was struggling with form and physically as well. The pace of the game had caught up with me and also my pains and aches were taking their toll. I used to really feel it when I tried getting out of bed the next day – the knocks I was sustaining were not recovering as fast as before. Due to some of the injuries I was carrying I had also lost some of my form. Fair enough, I was coming off the bench, but it did dent my pride a bit I must admit. It was time for a reality check – the team goal was a more important priority than my own personal agenda.

Consequently, I approached Rob with still about two years left on my contract and told him that I wanted to quit. It was on one of our long drives back from a game in London. It was tough for me to say it to him but I remember sharing my heart and saying that I wanted to leave. He wouldn't have any of it and said to wait a little while as he wanted to give me a fitting send-off. The following year he rested me to keep my enthusiasm going, which was an intelligent move as it really fired me up to play again.

For my last ever game for Newcastle the fans turned up to farewell me in droves. Jonny was the captain and I can remember him handing me the ball and saying, 'This is your time – go and take our team out.' It was a really moving experience when they played the Samoan national anthem following the announcement that this was my last home game. Afterward, I gave a speech to thank Newcastle for the past five years, but during it the mike blew out – probably God's way of telling me 'enough said'! As the fireworks display came to a close I remember turning and looking Rob Andrew in the eye and saying 'thank you'. Now I understood what he had meant when he said he wanted to give me a fitting send-off.

After my final match at Northhampton, after everyone had left, it was just Jonny and I in the change room. Both of us were really sad that we were parting company. I remember trying to cheer him up by saying, 'Come on, bro – it's not the end of the world.' I guess we had grown close because I could relate to the fame that was thrust upon him as a young man and I could empathise with his situation. I always advised him to have a balanced life and never to allow rugby to dominate him as a person. So let me end this account of my time at Newcastle with a word from my good friend Jonny Wilkinson.

Jonny Wilkinson
England's star fly-half

'With Inga there was no such thing as compromise – which is what I and the other players utterly respected about him.'

'I mean no disrespect to any of the other great players that I've played alongside, but my great friend Va'aiga Tuigamala was the main player that helped me when I first entered the game. His attitude helped shape and form my own. I found myself watching everything he was doing in matches or at training – totally enthralled by how he went about his business and played the role as the superstar yet at the same time was the greatest team player in the squad. In Inga's defence, I hasten to add, he never saw himself as the star and was truly a humble bloke.

'I first met Inga when I came straight out of school into senior rugby. He was one of the first people to come up and speak to me when I arrived at the Newcastle clubhouse. That first introduction from Inga helped calm my "new kid on the block" nerves. I was really stoked to have the club's most valuable player coming over and making the effort to talk to a "rookie". But that's how he was and how I remember him to be – always going out of his way to put other people at ease.

'Besides his impressive stature, there was a whole lot more to Inga than what immediately met the eye. For a start, there was his beaming smile. It was like it was a permanent expression he wore no matter how tense the situation was on the field or in the training sessions. Of course, with ball in hand the expression on his face was one of pure business and you didn't want to be on the receiving end of one of his tackles when he was in this mode. But at the same time he was enjoying everything he was doing. It wasn't just a job for him.

'Despite being a big lad he had superb movement off his feet and could perform some truly astonishing feats of offloading with one hand here, there and everywhere. As champions of the premier league in 1998 we played in the Sanyo Cup against the rest of the world. The first time I got the ball was about twenty metres out from the line and I threw a pass to Inga that was a bit too high. I thought I'd fluffed it but Inga jumped high to catch it and before he landed was able to swivel and beat the defender. He then moved into a gap that he had created by his movement in the air and went through. However, along the way he lost his balance and started to stumble. About three defenders converged on him, and as he fell he threw a one-handed pass out the back of his right hand with his head in the dirt. It went about ten metres to Alan Tait who took it and by then we were three against one and the try was a certainty. I was totally amazed and remember wondering how on earth he had done it. I just threw a ball to a guy that was not the best of passes but he was able to completely open up the game with a single movement. Myself, I'd been too busy standing there with my mouth hanging open to even think of getting involved in the support play. It took me about a minute of rubbing my eyes to get my head around what had just happened.

'I could probably blame him single-handed for the present state of my body because I would be lifted by watching him do something extraordinary and it used to inspire me to go out and do something more. From a competitive edge we used to help each other to go up and up and attain higher levels than we were capable of by ourselves. That's what good team-mates do for each other. However, as far as taking out the opposition, Inga gives me too much credit as I really didn't challenge him as he was the one renowned for the big hits, even though we used to get into some of the same tackles to rough up the opposition. In all fairness, he was about three stone heavier than me and very, very good at what he did. Of course, on the kicking side of things it would have been a totally different story.

'One time I remember Inga putting in a big hit on the South African Japie Mulder, which didn't come out right. Inga hit him well but came off worst and got concussed. He fell to the ground and stopped moving. It was raining heavily and there was water all around. Unfortunately, Inga's face came to rest in one of the puddles on the pitch. I didn't care that the play was carrying on and attended to him. I tried in vain to lift him but he was much heavier than me and I struggled. Luckily, Pat Lam came over and together we managed to roll him over. Thankfully, he was okay. Even though he needed to go off he was desperate to stay on. His drive to remain on the field that day demonstrated to me his courage. I learned from Inga that you didn't know how much you were capable of until you were prepared to give it a go.

'For a big guy, on the field Inga was a master of concealment: the opposition were fooled on a number of occasions into thinking they were in wide open spaces only to have Inga spring up out of nowhere and smash them. In a game we played against Bedford I remember him putting in a massive hit on one of their forwards from one of his trademark wide runs in from an angle. It made me just think that this Inga Tuigamala was on another level altogether. I knew then that he had won our personal competition by a mile.

'From Inga I learnt to give nothing less than my all and to leave my best on the field. Many professionals are more focused on a long career and afraid of letting it all out for fear of injury. But that's not how I want to be remembered. In terms of length of career, it may not be the best tactic to try to tackle everything that comes your way, but it hasn't stopped me. When you're on the field your decision to make the tackle is made for you by your internal or innate instinct

---

to compete and win. For me, sport is about living for that one moment and making it count. Watching Inga taught me that when you finish playing, all that you have is your reputation and how you played your game, which is how you create that reputation. The reality is that you can take time to build a good one but you can destroy it very quickly. Seeing him give his all during my formative years set the tempo for my own subsequent performances on the field.

'What makes a player amazing as opposed to just good is not just doing the great or amazing things, but doing them or trying to do them *every single time* that you're out there. When Inga was on the field it didn't matter if he was having his best game or not quite so good a game. It didn't matter, as the next second I always knew he was going to do everything he possibly could to turn things around. It's not like he did it one week and had a rest the next – he did it week in and week out. With Inga there was no such thing as compromise, which is what I and the other players utterly respected about him. That's one thing I live for in my own game – to give a hundred per cent and not compromise or hold back. His feats lifted the entire team.'

SAYING FAREWELL

'Inga has mentioned how his last appearance ever for Newcastle was an away game against Northampton. As I recall, we had no right to be in that game. The whole team was lifted by the occasion and followed Inga's example. He was awesome in that game and we fought to the end and came within a few points of winning. Naturally, it was a huge disappointment not to win, and it was also massively sad that Inga's time with us had come to an end. I wanted him to play forever. Sitting in the change room afterwards it finally dawned upon me that we wouldn't be sharing any more of those moments alongside each other on the field. There was going to be a big change and I felt that I was losing not just a fellow player but a friend – a friend who had been a massive inspiration to me from the beginning of my senior playing career. Rugby for me was never going to be the same again.

'I would say that Inga Tuigamala was maybe the single most inspirational sportsman that I have encountered on the playing field. He was certainly one of the few players who seemed able to create, use and maintain rugby as a *way of living* as opposed to just *making a living*. Together with his values and beliefs he has given so much to the sport both on and off the field. I guess me seeking out his counsel during the Lions tour of New Zealand in 2005 is testament to the impact that he had on my career. Catching up with him again in Auckland and having dinner with his family brought home to me how much I'd missed having him around over the years since his retirement. Being able to converse with him on a day-to-day basis kept me balanced and I found myself offloading a lot of rugby to him on that visit.

'Nowadays it's an extraordinary story in many respects as he has started up in business as a funeral director. If someone had said to me back in the Newcastle days that when Inga returned to New Zealand he would end up in this line of work, although I might have been surprised I would have honestly said that the role would be perfect for him. I say this because I know that Inga possesses the character, fortitude and personality to take on any role with the same dedication he used to display on the field of rugby, giving his best and nothing less.'

Jonny's reminiscing has jogged a few of my own memories so let me elaborate more on some of the incidents he has mentioned.

Firstly, let's go back to that Sanyo Cup game when he threw the pass to me that almost went into the stands. Perhaps Jonny thought I was eight feet tall? I recall that movement quite vividly as I caught the pass high above my head. Seeing the defender approaching quickly, I had to decide whether to take the tackle or avoid it. I chose to shimmy around him all in the one movement while I was airborne and then beat the approaching cover defence. As I was making for the line I was tackled and with my forward momentum whilst falling to the ground I was able to flick the one-handed pass to our approaching centre, Alan Tait, to score under the posts.

That hit from former Springbok Japie Mulder, when we played Leeds, I remember well also. I'd miscalculated my tackle on him and went in a bit too early. There was a massive clash of heads and I went down in a heap. Then all I could hear was a ringing sound blaring in my ears. As I was on the ground I could vaguely see the Leeds players high-fiving Japie for a job well done in taking me out. Our physio that day, Martin Brewer, told me that my game was over and that I needed to come off. In my dazed state I can recall saying to him, 'Don't you dare take me off the pitch or you will suffer the consequences later.' Poor Martin was obliged to capitulate.

In situations like these my former All Blacks team-mate Michael Jones would say:

'It's always better to give than to receive.'

Amen to that, brother Michael! On the rugby field I can be quite a generous bloke when it comes to giving it out to the opposition – all well within the rules of the game, mind you. So I went over to Jonny and told him to hold back as I wanted to 'open up the pocket'. In this case it was more appropriately 'opening up the snare for a Springbok'. Eventually, after Jonny had opened up his lines, I was able to get my 'payback' and show Japie what a generous guy I can be – although I admit that Jonny did chip in as well. Our generosity in the form of a number of telling hits eventually led to Japie capitulating, calling it a day and being replaced.

As for Jonny's parting comment on me and my present career, is he for real? If someone had told me while I was still playing that I'd wind up being a funeral director when I retired from rugby I probably would have responded, 'Mate, you must be joking!' Leastways, that's the most common response I get when people find out what I'm doing with myself these days. But that's for another chapter, so keep reading.

8.

Return to New Zealand

We must never cease our exploration, and the end
of all our exploring will be to return to the place
where we first began and to truly know that place
for the first time.

T. S. Eliot

L et me briefly revisit the time in my life when I had just made the All Blacks. I was sitting in the house of the late Mayor of Auckland, Mr Keith Hay, overlooking the Manukau Harbour, and he said to me, 'When are you at the happiest point of your life?' As a nineteen- or twenty-year-old at the time, I couldn't answer him. He pressed me to give him an example. So I answered, 'When you're successful.' With a smile the wise Mr Keith Hay replied, 'No, more than that, Inga.

'When you're in control of your destiny, that's when you will be the happiest.'

All along my life's journey I've tried to live out those wise words of advice. When I left the All Blacks I did not do so because I was down, but when I was on a high. I wasn't dropped by the selectors, but chose to leave of my own accord. When I left Wigan for Newcastle in 1997 for the most expensive union transfer for a player to that time, I did so on my terms. I left Newcastle in 2002 still with time to go on my contract. Again, it was all part of me taking a firm hold of my destiny. I had achieved the goals I'd set out to achieve in rugby and didn't want to prolong it any further. When I look back at the choices I've made, I have no feelings of regret but only satisfaction. I left on my own terms.

Some may have liked to think that I still had a few more years left in me to play, but I prefer to think otherwise. My philosophy has always been that the welfare of the team is the primary objective and not the individual's personal agenda. Sure, I don't deny that as a player you do have your own personal goals that you want to achieve, but in a sport like rugby they should always come second to the good of the team. At the end of my time at Newcastle I had reached the stage where I couldn't put my hand on my heart and honestly say that I could continue giving 100 per cent for the team. As you will have read, Jonny Wilkinson's perception of me was of a person who never held back – and that's the reputation I wanted to leave behind. We all need to take stock of our lives on a regular basis. Like the philosopher Socrates says:

'The unexamined life is not worth living.'

It was about taking a good hard look at myself and accepting it was time to move on.

The main sign for me that it was time to move on was that

my enthusiasm and excitement had faded. The butterflies had stop fluttering and I had started to lose my eagerness to go out and play. There were also the glaring physical indications that my playing days were numbered – the mounting aches and pains in my body. Even towards the end I started to develop arthritis in some of my joints and in the cold of England it took longer to warm up.

Could I perhaps have pushed myself and gone one more year? Yes, but would I have got any better? The answer is a firm no. A sportsperson needs to recognise when their time is up, and whilst I still possessed the strength and ability, the harsh reality was that my body was giving up on me. There were some offers from Australia, but at the time the only thing on my mind that mattered was getting my children back home to New Zealand and reintegrating them into life there. My mind was made up – it was time to hang up my boots.

We had ventured over to England with two children and now we were returning with four. As much as Daphne and I called New Zealand home, it was going to be totally foreign to them. Without doubt, it was a sad occasion for us as we had to say goodbye to all the friends we'd made over our time in England. It would be a while before I returned, and I remember sitting in the airport lounge on 14 May 2002 waiting for the final call to board and having it hit me that my rugby-playing career was really over. On coming to England it was always our intention that it was to be for only a short three-year stay, but it had ended up being nine years altogether.

There was definitely an air of uncertainty as to what awaited us when we arrived back in New Zealand. Now the curtain was brought down on my career, many questions ran through my mind. What am I going to do now? What am I going to get involved with now that my playing career is over? How will New Zealand embrace me? How will my children adapt to what is in effect a foreign country to them? As Daphne rightly points out later in this book, although the move to England was all about providing a better future for our children, our return to New Zealand was all about them too. We didn't want to deprive them any longer of contact with their wider family and learning more about their culture and identity as Pacific Islanders. I didn't want them to ever say later on that their parents didn't give them the chance to experience these important things. In the early days, my goal had been to only do better than my dad and own my house freehold. Yet I had achieved this and so much more. God had allowed me to go to England to prepare me to return to my homeland more mature and with a better outlook on life. I had grown more into my responsibility to my family and life in general.

New Zealand is a small place and the people didn't make a big thing of my return. That's the nice thing about New Zealand – if you're successful, great; if not, so what? From a lifestyle block we had bought out in Kumeu, West Auckland, we would all settle back into life in New Zealand. This was so that we could slowly get back into the city life because out in Newcastle we had lived in the country for almost five and a half years and wanted to retain that rural feel. One thing we were a bit apprehensive about, funnily enough, was what challenges the strong English accents our kids had developed would pose for them. However, while their cousins were intrigued by these

Island kids with their thick Geordie brogue, it didn't take those accents long to begin to disappear.

While the priority was settling the kids in, the big question in my own mind was what to do now, as I always like to be occupied doing something. It was clear though that first my body wanted to have a good rest. Meantime, Daphne was able to get a part-time job working at friend Tony Soljan's newly built café at his Kumeu winery. In fact, she ended up liking the café business so much that six months later she came to me saying that she wanted to open her own. So we scouted around and it wasn't long after that that we opened up Friends Café. It was Daphne's little baby and she enjoyed it for about two and a half years while we found our feet. After a while of me doing not much I knew that it was time to move on and come out of my 'retirement'. To tell the truth, I was getting bored – and there's only so much golf a man can play. The time had come to look around for something that I wanted to do.

Looking back on my sporting career, I acknowledge that I have played for some great teams: Auckland, the All Blacks, Samoa (league and rugby), Wigan and Newcastle. While my sporting accomplishments will forever be something I treasure, there is always more that one can attain in life. Recently, when a friend of mine stood up to introduce me before I spoke at an event he'd organised, he shared an observation he made when he came to my home to pick me up. He said that on entering the house he had expected to find photos, trophies or some other memorabilia of my playing days but was amazed to find that the only ones to be seen belonged to my sons and were not mine. This is because I have never been one to revel too much in my past successes. I always say to people that playing and achieving what I have done is an honour and privilege that humbles me for which I am grateful to God. In fact, I don't even have any of my past playing jerseys – last time I checked, those that hadn't been gifted to charity to help with fundraising were with my mum.

Anyway, I have always been a firm believer in giving something back and that was one of the major motivations for me starting my funeral business. It's my way of saying thank you to my people and giving something back to them. My good friend, former legend of Manu Samoa, and general manager of Tuigamala and Sons, To'o Vaega, will explain.

To'o Vaega
General Manager, Tuigamala and Sons Funeral Services

'What makes Inga such a well-respected person is that he's a straightforward guy and doesn't hold anything in – if he's not happy, he'll tell you.'

'One of my very first meetings with Inga was in 1996. At the time, Manu Samoa was touring the United Kingdom and we were preparing to play Ireland in a test match. Our coach Bryan "BG" Williams asked me in the lift of the hotel what I thought of the idea of Inga Tuigamala playing for Manu Samoa. Because of me being a senior player at the time, BG wanted to get my feedback. I remember him saying something to this effect: "I hope as one of the senior players you don't mind that I'm trying to get Inga Tuigamala to be a part of our team." I was pleasantly surprised as I knew that while Inga was still playing in league he was also on loan to Wasps. BG went on to say that he had spoken to Inga and that he was really keen to play for Samoa and was in the process of sorting out the necessary arrangements.

'The prospect of someone of Inga's high calibre playing in our team would only lift us. Also, for that particular tour we had some senior players pull out because the finances that were on offer were not what they fancied. Now we had one of the highest-paid Samoan rugby players prepared to forfeit part of his salary to come and play for the land of his birth. For this, my respect for and admiration of Inga really increased and I was sure that it would inspire the rest of the team. I had played against Inga many times at club level in Auckland and knew him to be a very formidable opponent. In fact, he'll laugh when I say that the night before the games I used to struggle to sleep! He was so quick off both feet and a very strong player to take down. I also played against Inga in 1993 when Manu Samoa took on the All Blacks at Eden Park in the very first test between the two sides. Other players with Samoan heritage in the New Zealand side that day included Michael Jones, Joe Stanley and Frank Bunce. Now having Inga line up alongside me as a team-mate was going to be a real blessing.

'BG and the rest of the management team called a meeting and it was like a court-case scenario. The rest of the players were not aware of what was happening as it had been kept a big secret until now. Then BG made the announcement and after a few seconds there was Inga walking into the room. Some of the boys had never met Inga before and they were a bit nervous to be around him. To them, Inga was a big-name All Black and league player they used to watch on TV back in Samoa, so they were a bit shy to approach him because of his "superstar" status. But Inga was not a guy to show off and immediately played down his standing by going to them and being the first to break the ice. Of course, they soon saw that he was a very humble person. Furthermore, Inga's professional attitude was invaluable to pass on to the younger players and even as a senior player I learnt a lot from him. He never looked for special treatment and was always prepared to submit himself to the team protocol.

'As part of the induction of all Manu Samoa players at the time, Inga was required to say which village he came from, and also say a little bit about himself as this was a necessary part of the team-bonding process. This was something new for Inga, who hadn't realised how close the team unit was. We go back to our roots like this because that is how we believe the Island family becomes close. That's what we wanted to maintain and also promote with the players – the family bond in the team. They needed to show how proud they were to wear the Manu Samoa jersey and be proud of representing their family, people and country. After the first game I got Inga to stand up and said to him that when you are new in the team you have to do a dance. I thought this might be too much to ask of him as many of the players that were not residing in Samoa had often refused. But not Inga – he did the dance as the team's new player. It was really uplifting to all of us to see that even though Inga had spent so much time away from Samoa he was proud to uphold his culture. He demonstrated to us that even though you may be regarded as the best player in the world, you can still be humble.

'I know that Inga was grateful for this emphasis on cultural values as these were the things that made him appreciate being a Samoan. I remember when I first made the Manu Samoa team it was required that the new players had to wait on the older guys – make them cups of tea and also serve them food. We had no choice and had to do it and respect them even though we may not have been too happy about it. Now that I was a senior player I didn't enforce the same regime but I maintained the important cultural appreciation.

'However, one thing I did take a stand on was a bad habit some of our foreign-based players picked up of using the word "bro" to refer to each other. That sort of slang word I didn't want to hear, so its use was outlawed. "We are not Kiwis or Aussies but Samoans," I admonished them. "If you want to call your team-mate something then refer to him as *uso* [Samoan for 'brother']." Inga was in total agreement. I always maintained that if you are with the Samoan team, then you do it the Samoan way. Doesn't matter where you were born, you're still Samoan.

'Inga was known as a Christian and appreciated that we used to have a team prayer together in the evenings – he loved this and said it made him feel that he was in the right family. Inga also commented that while he had enjoyed his time with the All Blacks his time with Manu Samoa was equally special. I'm grateful that after our tour I was able to get a contract in England and thus maintained my contact with him for a further time.

'When the press used to come up to us after the game we would always say thank you to our people. But now in our work as funeral directors I can see that what we do through this ministry is a far better way of showing appreciation to our people, by helping them in their time of mourning and deep distress. After placing the casket in the ground and returning to the office we feel really good that we have fulfilled our calling. When people come over and say that the deceased was a loyal supporter of ours in the Manu Samoa team we receive further confirmation that we are serving our people. They were the ones looking to us when we were representing our country and now we have a chance to farewell them with respect and dignity.

'Mind you, it's not only Pacific Islanders that we bury; there are many European people as well. The family comes in and they ask to meet Inga. It is usually then that they mention that when their recently deceased relative heard that Inga was a funeral director, they had requested to be looked after by him when they died. Why? Because they were a fan. Many is the time I have said to Inga that he's in the right business, and although people still question his decision I am sure that he was praying for God to show him the right work to go into. Whilst Inga says that he is not a brainy guy, I can see that he has a genuine love for people. I see plenty of people who have degrees who are not successful in business in the way that Inga is thanks to God's blessing.

'I have also grown to respect Inga even more now that his playing days are over as I see what a great family man he is. He truly has a heart for his family. What makes Inga such a well-respected person is that he's a straightforward guy and doesn't hold anything in – if he's not happy, he'll tell you. I see it when he is coaching his sons. He may be a bit hard on them but he tells them what he expects from them and how to behave, and never to show off.'

One of the stark realities of life that hit me right between the eyes on my return to New Zealand was the deaths of ten of my close friends who were from various ages, backgrounds and cultures. In attending their funerals and seeing how the different funeral homes attended to their funeral arrangements and managed the grieving processes for the families, memories of my father's funeral back in 1981 where I was mesmerised by the European undertakers and the way they walked and the funny hats they wore came flooding back. Growing up in a house that backed onto a cemetery where we used to play hide-and-seek, rugby and have a run-around had probably contributed to my fascination with the undertaking business too. Even more than observing that they were good at what they did, I saw an opportunity here to possibly do something meaningful with my life; to make a contribution for the betterment of society. In this role I was confident I could make a real difference to the lives of families in their difficult time. Here was the niche I'd been looking for and I wanted to embrace it.

9.

Tuigamala and Sons Funeral Services

Naked we come into this world
and naked we shall leave.
Job 1:21

Not being a person to jump headfirst into anything without proper research, I embarked on my little reconnaissance into the undertaking scene by looking through the various funeral homes listed in the Yellow Pages to see what I could learn about them. One particular advert featured a Pacific Island funeral director, so I got in touch and told him I was keen to come and have a look around and see how things were done. All was going well until he asked my name. When I introduced myself he replied, 'Good one, mate,' and put down the phone. When I promptly called back and he asked if I was saying that I was Inga the Winger he did the same. By now I was pretty frustrated and immediately rang back to say that I was happy for us to meet in the flesh to prove it wasn't a hoax. To cut a long story short, I went to work with him just to observe from a distance what was involved.

It was a fantastic experience that hooked me completely,

although at this stage I was just happy to work in the business and didn't have any intentions of owning one of my own. After some time this was to change. As I continued to observe and do more research I remember saying to Daphne that I could see this wasn't so much a business as a ministry through which I could see us making a real difference in people's lives. Her support of my vision was the final confirmation that this was to be our next calling.

To the sceptics, we were launching into an industry of which we had little prior experience. But our firmly held belief was that

> where God gave the vision,
> He would make the provision.

Whilst I didn't have the qualifications, I knew that God didn't call the qualified but that He qualified the called. A lifetime of schooling in the 'university of life' inspired me with the confidence to acquire the necessary skills. The finances that I had accumulated from rugby would get us started in something that would not only give us a return on our investment but the opportunity to give something back to the community. At the grand opening of Tuigamala and Sons Funeral Services, on 8 April 2006, more than 300 guests were in attendance.

However, in the beginning, I was under no illusions that my bold decision to become a funeral director was going to be warmly accepted by everybody. Let's be honest, it's definitely not everyone's cup of tea, but that wasn't going to deter me. A lot of hilarious remarks and comments flowed from family and friends when we first shared the news with them. Then when they noticed that we weren't laughing and were 'deadly' serious they began to ask the whys. Our response was, 'One day you will see why.' For some of them, I have had the sorrowful task of conducting the funeral arrangements for their loved ones. After the formalities are over many of them have come back to me and said, 'Inga, we truly appreciate you for what you are doing.'

When I shared my desire to open a funeral home with my friend Murray Deaker during a round of golf, he paused for a moment and then let out a roar of laughter. When I reminded him that he'd promised not to laugh at my announcement, he replied that he wasn't laughing *at* me but *for* me. Like Murray, after people get the initial shock of finding out what I'm doing out of their system, they realise the importance of this new direction in my life. Friends such as Jonny Wilkinson, Jason Robinson, Rob Andrew and the super-fast winger Martin Offiah have all seen the role as being my calling.

Martin Offiah
One of league's most prolific ever try-scoring wingers
'. . . he had the skills of a halfback, the body of a prop forward and the speed and sidestep of a winger.'

'I first learned that Inga had become a funeral director when I watched the IRB's weekly rugby show *Total Rugby*. The news was a bit out of left field but after it finally sank in

I thought to myself, "Yes, that job really suits his character and personality. It's a perfect match for the type of person he is."

'I came to know Inga really well in our playing days at Wigan and I have always known him to be a person who is very respectful, compassionate and caring – all attributes that are really important for any funeral director to have. On the field of rugby he was one of those very rare guys who would absolutely smash an opponent in a perfectly legal tackle, then turn around and be really genuinely concerned for their welfare afterwards and check on them to see if they were okay. However, back when it was announced to us that we had signed one of the world's best union wingers, I remember it made me feel a bit uneasy. The club's other winger at the time was Jason Robinson and he was in great form having just got his first cap for England. But I had just come back from an injury and was still recovering and not playing at my best. I remember thinking that my time could be up. I was glad that it wasn't, and together we went on to win some major trophies playing alongside each other for Wigan.

'I would always say to people that Inga was Jonah Lomu *before* Jonah Lomu. He was big in size for a winger but he was also fast – what I call a 'super-winger'. In school every boy feared playing against an opponent like him. At the same time you were very relieved if he was on your side. Even though Inga had the size, I noticed that he didn't use it the way some of the modern-day big wingers do. Sure, he could smash the opposition over with his size but he had other far more effective weapons in his playing arsenal: speed, agility, footwork. Plus there were other attributes that I wasn't used to seeing in someone of his size and stature. Along with the silky hands of a world-class number nine or ten, he had the passing skills of a halfback, the body of a prop forward and the speed and sidestep of a winger. With that variety of talents, he was the complete player.

'For a big man he was also very humble – even his tone of voice reflected his humility. At the same time he was always able to have a laugh and dispel the perception that if you are serious you cannot have fun. I also remember him being a good basketball player. I used to enjoy having a game with him and Henry Paul, which is where I think they mastered the one-handed overhead pass they used to execute so often in rugby. Off the field, I remember him sitting in the physio room reading away at his Bible and being peppered with questions from some of the players intrigued by his faith. Every so often, the guys used to put that faith to the test, but I have always known him to stay rock solid. On one occasion there was a pretty girl walking past the team bus which got almost the entire team to stop and take a look, and then they turned their attention to Inga to see what his reaction would be, if he would look at her. Of course, being Inga, he didn't bat an eyelid. I know that he was really instrumental in Jason Robinson's turnaround for the better. To me, it was as if Jason had transformed overnight and it was testimony to the positive influence of this man.'

FROM ME TO YOU ABOUT INGA

- Inga always played within the rules of the game: he was never someone to go out to injure the opposition deliberately.

- Inga was an old-fashioned knight in a rugby player's body: he would not lower himself to conquer and would always maintain his dignity and integrity on the pitch.

- Inga is a family man, a peaceful and gentle but strong giant.

- Inga possesses a rare quality: the ability to galvanise a room just by his sheer presence.

'What Inga Tuigamala had was an "X factor", a certain something that inspired the team. I count myself blessed that my career coincided with his and I had the opportunity to play alongside him.'

'A knight in a rugby player's body', eh? That's the first time anyone's ever called me that. Now, I have been on the park with some really speedy fellows in my day, but Martin Offiah's speed was an exception to the rest. The day my good friend Craig Innes joined Leeds, Martin celebrated by scoring a record ten tries against them! Chatting with Craig after the game he was utterly amazed at the talent and speed Martin possessed. Craig was no slowcoach himself, but Martin was able to run around him with ease that day.

Even during sprint drills at our training sessions Martin used to make it seem like we were running in slow motion. I can remember him teasing us after eighty metres of our 100-metre dash by running backwards to finish off – and he would still beat us! Martin 'Chariots' Offiah was an Olympic sprinter who somehow found his way onto the rugby field instead of the running track. He truly set the rugby league world on fire with his tremendous pace and ability. His nickname 'Chariots' came from the movie *Chariots of Fire*. In fact, Martin and his name are the reasons the crowds in England used to sing 'Swing Low, Sweet Chariot'.

Never allow others to extinguish the flame and passion you have in your heart to fulfil your calling in life. Don't deprive this world of the talent you possess to make it a better place. Some of you may be in a job that you feel isn't your calling, but it's never too late to make the move to do what you know you are called to do. Look at and learn from my example. Do you know how much flak I copped from my peers and the public for doing what I'm doing now? What was *your* first reaction when you heard that Inga Tuigamala had become a funeral director? Admit it, you probably thought that I'd lost my mind, didn't you?

Even though I have had the unenviable task of burying my friends' and family's babies, siblings, grandparents, parents, do I regret the vocation I have chosen? Never! I see it as a genuine calling (interestingly, the word for vocation is derived from the Latin 'vocare', which means 'calling'). So for me I believe that I have found in my role as a funeral director my God-given calling. The point that I want to highlight is that to truly fulfil one's calling in life may require moving beyond what others expect and breaking the mould that this world tries to put us all in. I'm the first to admit that I wasn't really sure of what I was getting myself into. Shouldn't I have just done what most sportspeople do when they retire – go into coaching or sports commentary?

In my line of work I see rich people, fools, the corrupt get honoured. I see bad people recognised above the good. I see people take their lives unexpectedly, toy with life without any consideration for dangers. Kings, queens, young, old, good and bad, rich and poor, all end up in the same place. When we die there is no more planning to be done. All planning ceases. We can't say tomorrow or next month we will do this or that. There are no more 'what ifs' or 'if onlys'. When you die it is all done and dusted. The obvious truth that has been underlined for me as a funeral director is that you never know when your life will end. There are many uncertainties in this world, but death is the one certainty that awaits us all. So don't take your unfulfilled dreams and ambitions with you to the grave. Do what you can do now as you don't know what tomorrow will bring. There is a poem that sums this sentiment up for me:

The Clock of Life

The clock of life is wound but once
and no man has the ability
To tell when the clock may stop,
Now's the only time you own,
Live, love, toil with a will, place no faith in tomorrow
For then the clock may be still.

Now that we are three years into the funeral business I must admit that it has been very satisfying. I also laugh at how things were when we first opened – there we were twiddling our thumbs and waiting anxiously for people to call, but after two weeks still there was no one. Then Daphne realised it was because we had done no advertising. That was just typical of how naïve we were back then, thinking that people would just come strolling through the door. With the advantage of experience, I appreciate the importance of having good, solid, clear systems. My business coach taught me this great acronym for S-Y-S-T-E-M:

Save   Yourself   Stress   Time   Energy   Money

Making the big move into my own business teaches me new things each day. That's why I like to encourage others to do the same and make the move beyond where you are at the moment. Don't allow others to dictate to you what you should or shouldn't do. You will never know the joy of experiencing distant lands if you keep your feet firmly planted on the shoreline. Step out in faith like Peter did when Jesus invited him to walk on water. Okay, Peter from the Bible only managed to walk for a short moment before he began to sink and Jesus had to rescue him – so, looking at this example, many people say that he failed. I beg to differ. There were eleven bigger failures back there in the boat. Of the twelve disciples, only Peter was prepared to step out of the boat.

Likewise, you will never know what you are capable of if you're unwilling to step out of your comfort zone. So often in life we get can get stuck in our mundane everyday routines and wonder why we don't experience life to its fullest. Could it be that we're not prepared to step into the unknown? Stepping into the funeral business was my 'walking on water' experience. Like Peter, I knew that if it didn't succeed I always had the loving hands of my God to reach out and save me. Not wanting to spiritualise things too much here, I want to encourage you to be prepared to step out in faith for the things that you really believe you are called to do as well. Initially it may be frightening, but don't allow fear to keep you in that boat.

Sure, it can be scary venturing into the unknown. It was for Daphne and me when we first left New Zealand for England, but we can both attest that the move overseas and now into our own business have been huge growth opportunities. Yes, I do admit that by stepping out of your comfort zone you run the risk that you may not succeed, but even then you can learn from the experience and move on. Remember, it's not so much failing at something that shapes you, it's more how you respond to it. Mark Twain offers the example of the man who learns a lot about cats by reading about them, but another man who learns twice as much about cats by pulling one's tail. Now that's me. I've always chosen to obtain my knowledge by direct means – from the university of life.

So always be prepared to give yourself a chance in life and give something a go. I was under no illusions that my rugby career would last forever. In due course, my life will come to an end as well. When I die I want to know that I have run my race and given it my all. You too have been created with a multitude of qualities and abilities, so don't let them go to waste.

10.

Culture, Faith and Community

Perhaps the greatest social service
that can be rendered by anybody to this country
and to mankind is to bring up a family.

George Bernard Shaw

It is my belief that as parents we have a responsibility to hand on the baton of cultural pride to our future generations. When I say pride, I'm not talking about trying to place one culture above any other, but more about an appreciation and respect for who you are and where you have come from. Our wish to be able to instil in our children the great culture that we have both been brought up in was one of the main reasons for our return to New Zealand.

Playing for Manu Samoa, as you will have read in To'o Vaega's contribution in Chapter 8, presented me with the chance to learn more about and to be immersed in my Samoan culture. At that time in 1996 I was still on loan with Wasps and Manu Samoa was touring the United Kingdom. They were struggling for players as some of their senior members couldn't make the tour. Coach Bryan 'BG' Williams and captain Pat Lam decided to approach me to see if I would be keen to join the squad. It was a move that worked in their favour and at the same time gave me the chance to give back something to the land of my birth, Samoa. However, first I needed to seek dispensation from Maurice Lindsay who was chairman of the English Rugby Football League board. Fortunately, he granted the official release that allowed me to take the field for Manu Samoa on that tour.

We had an incredible victory over Ireland in my first test for Samoa where I started on the wing and helped set up two tries. There were some wonderful celebrations after that surprise win over the more favoured Irish team. The other memorable victory in my time with Manu Samoa was against the Welsh Dragons at the 1999 World Cup in England. Graham Henry was the coach for Wales and they were on a twelve-game winning streak. We had the unenviable task of playing them in front of their home fans at the Millennium Stadium in Cardiff and were obviously the underdogs.

In preparation for this game, Pat Lam, Stephen Bachop, To'o Vaega, BG and the rest of the coaching staff sat around the table looking at ways to tame this rampant Welsh side. Pat knew Graham Henry quite well and from there we were able to put together a game plan to extinguish the Dragons' flame. The strategy was executed to a tee earning us a well-deserved win against the Welsh, who incidentally were Five Nations victors going in to that particular tournament. The highlights for me were us tackling our hearts out for the full 80 minutes and Pat scoring a length-of-the-field intercept try to secure the victory.

We didn't make the quarter-finals that time round, but without a doubt it was a moment to savour and gave Wales along with the rest of the rugby-playing nations a huge shock. The message we sent was: 'Underestimate us at your peril!' Graham Henry, who in my book is the ultimate professional, gave us our dues in offering his congratulations after the win. The redoubtable Pat Lam has his own reflections to offer on our playing days together.

Pat Lam
Former Manu Samoa captain and current Auckland Blues coach

'Who would have thought these two Samoan boys would have both ended their playing days up here in the North of England?'

'Our paths first crossed when Inga was selected for the New Zealand Secondary Schools team (in those days he still sported his big afro). The training sessions were usually an hour and a half long, but with Inga there we went an extra hour as he was unfamiliar with the drills. Naturally, we were none too impressed and thinking, "What's up with this guy?" – who was bigger than your usual winger – and we began to question his selection in the team. That weekend he totally amazed us and more than justified his inclusion by scoring five tries – "Oh, okay then," we thought, "he's not that bad so maybe he can stay!"

'Inga and I played together for the Auckland Colts when Graham Henry was coach. It was the Under 21 team and it was usually premier club players that were selected. It was unusual for us schoolboys to be selected, so a few eyebrows were raised when Graham plucked me, Inga and Craig Innes straight out of school to play for the Colts. We ended up playing together for the Auckland senior team too, and also played against each other in 1994 when I played for Manu Samoa and Inga played for the All Blacks before he went off to England to take up league.

'Our paths didn't cross again until 1996 when I was captaining Manu Samoa and BG Williams was our coach. We were heading up to the United Kingdom for a game against Ireland. At that time union had just gone professional and we had learned that Inga was on loan with Wasps. We reasoned that since he was playing union for them, then he might be interested in appearing for Manu Samoa. Also, the other thing that was in our favour was that back then you could still play for more than one international team. This brainstorm led to BG approaching Inga to consider representing Manu Samoa and ultimately pulling it off.

'Inga joined the team when we flew into the UK and it was a huge boost for all of us who were a part of that Manu Samoa squad. Earlier in this book Inga talked about how his time in England caused him to grow both on and off the field of rugby. When we met up again I had to agree – I was pleasantly surprised at how much my old friend had developed as a person. Not only had his fitness and physique improved out of sight but his new personal maturity was quite evident, and I credit that to him leaving behind his comfort zone in New Zealand for England. The cheeky laugh and infectious humour that we had grown to expect from him was exactly the same though!

'Even though union was slowly turning professional, most of the Manu Samoa team was still amateur. Having Inga in the side helped improve their game a lot as they were able to learn from him and he slotted in naturally. The key thing he showed the guys was that despite all the money and the high profile, he was a good Samoan boy at heart, filled with humility and respect. His faith and his personality galvanised the team on that tour, while for me it was great to sit around and catch up on the times since we had been together.

'Not only was the game against Ireland a really big one for us but it was our first appearance at the famous Lansdowne Road stadium. It was a great achievement to win so convincingly. Afterwards I was approached by Rob Andrew to play for Newcastle. As Inga was already playing professionally I took advice from him. He put me onto his agent to handle the contract and that concluded my move. Being my first professional contract, it was made even sweeter when two weeks after signing I found out that Inga was going to play with Newcastle too.

'As Inga rightly recalls, in 1997 Newcastle was in the second division and in our first year with them we won it and got promoted, following that up the very next year by winning the premiership – a feat no other club had ever achieved before. Off the field, our time in Newcastle was a great one for our families. Our children are all of similar ages and they got on very well together. The Tuigamalas were already settled into English life and their move to Newcastle was only from Wigan within the North of England. For the Lams making the big move from New Zealand, it was great having them around to help us with the transition. More than just being able to joke with each other, we were able to maintain some of our culture, and most importantly *eat* like Pacific Islanders at our many traditional get-togethers.

'As players we always appreciated Inga's inspirational presence in the change room before the games and at halftime – especially when we travelled away to some tough venues such as Leicester or the cauldrons of France. One of the biggest impacts he had on me was when we lost a European Cup semi-final against Agen. Rightly or wrongly, the coaching staff laid the blame for that loss squarely on Inga and me. For some unexplained reason (maybe they wanted to isolate our moaning?), Inga and I were roomed together for the following away game. This was very unusual as normally a back and a forward were not roomed together. Little did I realise this was going to turn out to be a really important moment for me.

As Inga and I started talking about that semi-final loss he suggested we open up a Bible devotion and hear what God had to say on the matter. After contemplating a verse that said

we were not to be conformed to the world
but transformed by the renewal of our minds,

I realised that I needed to change my attitude and not worry about what others thought. It was God who gave us the ability to play and it was for Him that we were to play. A massive weight immediately lifted from me and I went onto the field really pumped and played my heart out in the next game, receiving the man of the match award against Bristol that day. When the TV interviewers asked what had happened to turn me around from the disappointing loss of the previous game I just smiled and acknowledged the hand that God had played. That message has stood with me since then and I am forever grateful to Inga for what he shared in that word to me.

'I am also especially proud that Inga is a fellow Samoan and that he is never ashamed of who he is. He was and still is a huge role model for all us Pacific Islanders, shining in whatever he does. I pay tribute to Inga as being someone who has been blessed mightily by God. I say this in light of how far he has progressed in life. The key thing that I have observed about him is that he is not a selfish person. He has used his talents to benefit others. Even in England he was always opening doors for other Pacific Islanders. He was hugely instrumental for many Pacific Islanders playing in the United Kingdom and did a lot of work behind the scenes. All that he asked in return was for them to work hard and keep the door open for others in the same way he had done for them.

'After a stint for Northampton I was able to return to Newcastle and finish my career in England together with

Inga, where I had started off. Newcastle put on a tremendous farewell for us done in true Pacific Island style with all our favourite types of food and festivity. Inga and I were really impressed and at the same time humbled by the way the club had embraced us. Who would have thought these two Samoan boys would have both ended their playing days up here in the North of England?'

When Pat talks about 'keeping the door open for others' I emphasised to the guys that it was important that the way they conducted themselves with any club they played for needed to fit with our values. Not only were they to work hard and be respectful, but when they left the club it needed always to be on good terms and with proper humility and grace. By their conduct they were to ensure that the path for the next Pacific Island guy to come along was made smoother, and so on and so on, like a domino effect.

In his role as 'GM' (Grand Master) for Manu Samoa, To'o Vaega had a wonderful saying that summed up the importance and privilege of our shared heritage:

'Wherever you are in the world, you will know that you are Samoan by the way that you talk, walk, sit and play.'

Culture

In March 2007 a significant milestone in my life occurred. I was chosen to receive a high chief or 'Matai' title as it is known in my culture. Being selected by your family clan to receive such a title is a huge honour which comes with much responsibility. Whereas in some cultures it is usually the eldest sibling that receives the title, in Samoan culture it is left to the discretion of the family elders to choose whom they feel is fitting to receive it.

My father's family had approached my mother many years earlier for me to receive the title, but in her wisdom my mother refused it at the time as she realised that, with all the other commitments I had, it would not be possible for me to diligently undertake a role which involves cultural ceremonies, funerals and celebrations along with the day-to-day running of one's usual family affairs. A conservative estimate of my clan size could be in the region of two to three thousand members. So I guess Jason Robinson wasn't too far off the mark when he said that he thought I had 'a few million cousins'!

However, after many discussions with elders and close family members it was finally decided the time had come for me to accept the rightful title my own father had received in 1953. So 'Tuigamala Va'aiga Lealuga Tuigamala II' was the title with which I was invested. The other title I received – 'Fesolai' – was from my mother's side. There was both excitement and mystery wrapped up in having to go to Samoa for the traditional Pacific Island ceremony 'Kava' in the very village, Sa'anapu Lotomua, where my father was invested with his chiefly title. Local and district chiefs gathered from all around to acknowledge that

I was now one of the leaders and explain to me the traditional protocol and culture. Enormous preparations took place behind the scenes to make it all happen. We had to feed and provide for a lot of people and to acknowledge my father's family who had come from New Zealand and Australia and as far afield as the United States of America to be there.

After my father's death in 1981 I had not been very closely connected with his family. To have finally received this title was of immense significance for what was to come, laying a huge platform for my future family involvements and taking my responsibilities to a whole new level. One moment I was playing rugby on the other side of the world, now I was faced with making decisions that would affect many other people in their daily lives. It really made clear to me the saying 'charity begins at home'. Now I felt more connected than ever to my culture and my people.

There is a Samoan proverb:

'E tele atu a'a ile aiga ole tagata, lo'o a'a ole la'au.'

Roughly translated this means: 'There are more roots in a man's family than the roots of a tree.' Even though I had a good appreciation of being a family-orientated person, now in my role as high chief it took on a far deeper meaning. There was now so much more required of me, or, as the Good Book says:

'From those to whom much is given,
much will be required.'

Given that it is part of my daily duties to ensure that there is harmony, unity and love shared amongst all members of my clan, mediating disputes, attending funerals and weddings and celebrations, I see the relevance of that biblical teaching now more than ever before.

Some might feel that with the already complex lifestyle I lead this additional responsibility is all too much for me to handle. They should know by now that I never take on anything unless I am justly able to fulfil what is required of me. While I must again say that I am deeply honoured to have been given these responsibilities and embrace my chiefly role with pride and respect for my people, if there is one thing I wish to emphasise it is that I never sought after it. It was not my life ambition or something that I pursued for my own glorification. Instead, I believe that it was bestowed upon me in recognition of what dwells within me.

Perhaps there is a parallel with my receiving the high chief title in the Hebrew story about King David. The story goes that when David stood with his father Jesse and God confirmed that here stood the next King of Israel, Samuel began to question if his youngest lad was indeed the right choice. God responded:

'I the Lord do not see as man sees.
Man sees the outward appearance
but I the Lord see the heart of a man.'

I take from this that whilst others may look at you and see nothing much, God looks at you and sees the potential that He has placed within you. When others saw a shepherd boy, God saw in David a King. How true it is, and I believe that this applies to all of us as well. We must never allow what others think of us to discourage us from pressing ahead and becoming all that we can become. Doubters have featured all along the sidelines of my own life's journey. I just chose to never believe the garbage that they were spouting and pressed forward undeterred.

Of course, the other inspiring part of David's life is his famous encounter with Goliath. There are many lessons I learn from it:

1. When David approached Goliath he did so alone. In life we must be prepared to face our giants alone also; if not, we cannot conquer them. Likewise, if David had allowed the sceptics to get the better of him, he would never have defeated the giant.
2. We must be prepared to carry on striving despite the criticism of others. Again, I have faced my own fair share of criticism but never allowed it to stand in the way of my dreams.
3. David knew what his purpose was and he stuck to it until it was achieved. To achieve in life everyone needs commitment to a purpose, which is why I believe that

people fail not because their *problems are too big*, but because their *purpose is too small.*

These are the messages that I like to share with my children as well. As much as I want to make a difference in the world, I believe it starts right in my own house with my family. To be really effective, before I can make a difference in the world I need to first make a difference to them. That's why I have asked my son Jordan to share his thoughts on his father.

Jordan Tuigamala
Inga and Daphne's eldest child
'One of the great things about my dad is that he always makes the time to spend quality time with us . . .'

'When we were at Wigan and Newcastle my main memories are of being in the club crèche when Dad was playing and therefore I can't remember much of his playing days. However, later on as I grew up and we would look back at his games on video my siblings and I were amazed at the awesome things he used to achieve on the field. What I have really fond memories of from England are the lovely Christmas parties we used to put on. They were held in hire halls because of the great number of people that were invited. There was entertainment for all us youngsters with a bouncy castle and many other fun things for the kids inside. We thoroughly enjoyed them and it was good to get together with all Mum and Dad's friends, who became our extended family in England.

'There are times when being famous can have its drawbacks and some people may think that it's tough being the child of a famous sportsman, but for me it was not. Sure, Dad did attract a lot of attention. At these times I would admire him for the grace with which he used to handle the autograph hunters. He was polite in asking for space to be with his family yet at the same time obliging by signing them. We always understood because we knew that it came with the territory of being a rugby icon so we didn't mind at all. One of the great things about my dad is that he always makes the time to spend quality time with us, so I guess that's part of the reason we didn't really mind.

'My dad has taught me many things about life from the way he lives his. I am very grateful to him as he didn't force me to play rugby and expect me to become a superstar at what he was good at. For some kids there can be pressure having a father who has achieved so much through sport and then feel the burden that you have to do the same. My dad was not like that and he left us to find out what we wanted to do. I appreciate him for that as he was considerate of our needs and never wanted to smother us. Currently my brother Vaise and I have taken to amateur boxing and we are enjoying it. Dad takes us to training and even joins in with us in the early-morning sessions. This is what I mean when I say that he makes the time and is always participating in our lives.

'I see my dad around people and I observe that he treats others with respect and tries his best for everyone. At times I see that it takes a toll on him and results in him coming home really tired. He is unselfish and puts others first because it has a lot to do with his faith. This is why he started the funeral business and has recently undertaken a community centre project where he has provided premises for a gym.

When we see him on TV interviews he doesn't put on a public front that is different to how he is at home. That's how he is and he's exactly the same when he gets back home. My dad places God first in all that he does. He provides us with so much wisdom and guidance through his example. Some of the other important qualities for life that I have learnt from him are:

- How to carry myself in front of people.

- To always be considerate of others and stay humble.

- Never to be ashamed of my faith. (I remember him advising me before starting school, "Jordan, don't be ashamed to pray before you eat at school," and "Remember that you are a child of God."

'For us as his children we truly appreciate what he does and the time and effort he makes to be with us. This is how a family should be. It is true what he has said at the beginning of this book that children spell love, T-I-M-E. Yes, sure we have been given many presents by him, but I also agree that it is not the presents but his presence that really matters. Seeing how my dad has raised us and the time and care that he has put into being a good father, I thank the Lord for his example. When I become a father I want to do exactly what he has done for us.'

I am really proud of all my children. As parents it is so important that we set a good example for them to follow. Sadly, statistics prove that our children will be equally likely to follow a bad example as well. This is why it's so important to make the time to spend with them and be the best role model you can possibly be. If you don't, then someone else will step into that role, someone that may not share the same values as you. Don't leave it to the TV or computer games to raise your kids, you do it!

Faith

Allow me to add to what I shared with Jordan about the importance of not being ashamed of one's faith. I acknowledge my good friend, Michael Jones, for impressing this upon me through rugby as well. As doubtless many of you will know already, Michael Jones made a firm stand for God through his gift of playing rugby and did not play on Sundays. He took it a step further by wearing a wristband with a cross on it while playing.

I recall asking him what it represented when we played together for the Auckland rugby team. He explained that he used it as a reminder of his faith on the field and as a symbol of God's presence so that he knew he was never alone. Knowing this helped him to focus better on the game. It was a way for him to demonstrate his faith rather than just talk about it. More importantly, it was a constant reminder to him as to why he was playing in the first place: to glorify God.

For the same reasons, I followed Michael's example and decided to wear the wristband with the cross whenever I played.

Many others also followed that example and this practice of faith has gone on to inspire a whole new generation of Christian athletes to openly proclaim their faith.

At Wigan, the same question I initially asked Michael Jones, Jason Robinson enquired of me: 'Why do you wear a cross on your wristband?' I gave Jason the same answer that I was given. Jason went on to surprise me as we were lining up before a game when he showed me that he had on two wristbands with the cross. He joked that it was one more than me so that meant God would protect him twice as much. I just laughed and joked back that seeing as he was half my size he needed two, one was enough for me. We all have freedom of choice and I don't expect others to share my belief, but I was quietly pleased that he too was willing to show his faith in the same way. That cross on my wrist was a reminder of the price that my Saviour Jesus had paid for me and the duty I was under to show character worthy of my calling in whatever I do.

By living out my faith in public and not attempting to cover it up, there were always going to be people asking me about it – be they supporters, fans or the media. Rugby league was renowned for players having a mongrel, dog-eat-dog attitude, so for one of their own to stand up and be a witness for Jesus was something out of the ordinary. Coupled with my conduct on the field which enabled me to walk away from receiving a big tackle with no ill feelings, I became known as a person who stood up and lived out his faith.

I don't want to create the impression that I'm some kind of saint. There are times in the heat of the battle when you can easily lose your cool because you're being tested physically and emotionally by the opposition. On occasion guys have gone out to deliberately maim me which did not make me too happy. Then, at the point of raising my hand and clenching my fist to throw a punch at an opponent, I'd see the cross right there on my wrist and it would stop me dead in my tracks. The cross allowed me to look beyond my limited self for strength in order to overcome my frail humanity in the midst of such challenges and trials.

There are times when I have been criticised for being quite overt about my faith and people have tried to silence me for it. But how can I be silent when Jesus died openly and in full view of everyone that was around him on that cross on the hill of Calvary? It never fails to amaze me that people don't bat an eyelid if you're into any other religion, but if you say you're a born-again Christian, a follower of Jesus Christ, they freak out. Preconceived ideas rob people of the truth and simplicity of following Jesus.

My words of advice would be to pick up a Bible – get a modern translation – read the words of God, read about life and death and what happens afterwards. As I've stated, I was under no illusions that my rugby career would eventually be over. In due course both my life and yours will come to an end. When I die I want to know that I'm right with God, don't you?

Community

More than just having a title as chief of my family, I want to be able to make a difference to all those around me. At the moment there are many needful things that the West Auckland community where I live requires. We all know about the trouble young people can get into when they are not adequately engaged. Sport is a great medium to engage the youth and this is the avenue I want to make more accessible to young people today. This is why I have opened up a health and fitness centre for the greater West Auckland community that is located in the suburb of New Lynn.

This centre has been equipped with a boxing club where young men can learn some good lessons about commitment, discipline and respect; about the need to make drastic changes, set new goals, and, if applicable, be able to create new boundaries. It is my desire through this project with Michael Jones to help them make something better of their lives and show them that their destiny is in their own hands. Also, to cast off the shackles that limit their possibilities through possessing a negative mindset.

For it is the limits of our mindset
that determine the boundaries of our future.

Basically, teaching young people about life skills and their responsibility, identity and sense of belonging is about them knowing that their value in life is not determined by anyone else; about giving them self-worth and thereby promoting respect for themselves and others while helping them to make wise choices for their lives. One such area of wise choice is in the realm of friends.

Having the right friends around you is vitally important.

There is more peer pressure amongst the younger generation than ever before, so it is important for them to understand how crucial it is to surround themselves with the right type of friends. What I stress to my children is that outside of their family the influence of their friends is really critical to them building a successful life. The people you hang around with will either help shape you or break you. Those who help shape you and assist you to grow in life are the ones you call your friends, and those who are breaking you through putting you down or leading you into bad habits are definitely not your friends. A great saying that spells out very clearly the reflection friends make on us goes:

'Show me who your friends are
and I'll tell you who you are.'

I can certainly remember giving my mum a headache on this very subject. I was always having friends coming over and hanging about our house. One day Mum sat me down and gave me the following valuable lessons on choosing among friends:

1. There are friends who will be your friend in front of you but will be stabbing you behind your back. These are the type that when you're in trouble will run a mile and leave you to face it by yourself.
2. There are the 'passing hand friends'. They're the friends you'll see on the road as you pass them by who you raise your hand to say hi to.
3. There are the friends that take up a lot of your time. They

just love to drain all the energy out of you. These are HMP (High Maintenance People) friends – watch out for this type.

4. Finally, there are real friends who stick closer to you than a brother. If you have friends like that (which Mum doubted I had at the time), they will stick by you through the good times and the bad. They will hold you accountable and also point you in the right direction if they see that you're going off the track.

Who we choose as friends is really important. Ultimately the people you keep in your company or those you associate with often will influence you for good or bad. It's like the old saying that I learnt growing up:

All it takes is for one rotten apple
to spoil the rest of the apples in the basket.

Recently I came across this funny description of what a friend should not be:

What do you get when you cross a rescue dog
with a pit bull terrier?
You get a dog that will bite your face off
and then run along to go get help for you.

True friends are definitely not like that. They remain loyal no matter what the circumstances. Here is a story from the Bible that shows the qualities of true friends:

> While Jesus was teaching to a packed house there
> was a paralytic man carried in on his bed by his
> friends. Because of the huge crowds they could
> not easily reach Jesus. Through their commitment
> and sheer dedication to see their paralysed friend
> receive help, they persevered and went up on the
> rooftop and lowered him down through the tiles
> before Jesus. When Jesus saw their faith
> He healed the paralysed man.

I am really taken aback by the lengths to which these friends went in order to get help for their paralysed mate, exhibiting the 'three Cs' of true friendship:

1. Committed: True friends are committed to helping you no matter what the price to pay.
2. Concerned: True friends, despite ridicule and embarrassment from the 'crowds', will help you because they are concerned for your well-being.
3. Caring: True friends are caring. They put the needs of others before theirs and are always prepared to go to great lengths. No task is too hard to bear for their friend.

I recall an occasion when I had to practice the 'three Cs'. It was with my friend, the talented boxer, David Tua. It was when he was going through a tough time. I could have easily found a million excuses why I could not be there with David as he faced those tough times. I could have avoided the situation and turned a blind eye – but I am glad I didn't. That's not what a true friend would do. At great sacrifice to me and my family, I was there with him in the heat of his battle to render advice and moral support. Some of my other friends couldn't understand why I would put myself through all that strain and stress when it was not even my fight. What they didn't realise was that if it was them in David's place, I would have done the same.

I believe we all have a responsibility to be there for our friends who get injured on the battlefield of life; to be prepared to carry them off, ensuring that you leave no one behind! We need to make sure that they get the support and encouragement to get by safely. To me, that's what being a true friend is all about.

I am truly grateful that I have many friends who are like brothers to me. These are indeed the type of friends that are hard to come by. They will prop you up when you are down and are never a burden to have around. They are genuinely sincere as well as being great to hang out with.

Young people especially need to be wise in how they select the people that they associate with. I am grateful to my mum for the lessons she gave me on how to go about choosing my friends. I know that youngsters don't like to listen to the older people but this is something that needs to be done for two simple reasons:

1. Life is too short to learn from your own mistakes, so learn from others.
2. Avoid the pain that comes from making a mistake by learning from someone who has already experienced it.

In essence, the advice is for young people to speak to those who have been around longer than themselves on what they think about the friends they keep. Having the right type of friends around you creates an environment that will cause the seed of your potential to flourish and grow. The wrong type will be like life-choking weeds, depriving you of the sustenance to thrive.

Most of the time we pride ourselves on the freedom to express ourselves that comes with living in a lovely country like New Zealand. However, what we fail to realise is that with this liberty comes responsibility. We live in a world where we have to be mindful of what we say and to whom we say it. At the outset of this book I assured the reader of my honesty and truthfulness in the pages ahead. Part of my commitment to the community and especially to my Pacific Island people is for me to be a voice for them in New Zealand. I believe in always going to the head to sought matters out. Nevertheless, many people were shocked and wanted to know why I made a public stand for the National Party in 2008.

On that topic, let me say that for too long I have seen my people's voice silenced in this land of Aotearoa. The majority of the time that we are heard of is when Pacific Islanders are involved in crime or some other negative activity. I have become sick and tired of it. That's why I decided during the last general election to make my stand for change a public one. I could easily have exercised my right to keep my vote a secret, but I wanted it to go public.

It is my opinion that there must be a willingness from my people to embrace a change of mindset in order for their progress in this land. I say this in light of policies developed over the years that have resulted in keeping the masses dependent on the government for handouts or what we have commonly come to call 'benefits'. If people have the ability to work then the right choice, I feel, is for them to set the right example and work. I see no need for them to have to continue receiving government handouts. They need to be encouraged to come *off the benefit* and *become a benefit*. You become a benefit to your family and society by getting into employment and earning your money, thus being a good role model to those around you.

For me, that role model (and my hero) is my mum. When my dad died, Mum was left with fourteen children to raise. That was no easy task, especially more difficult for her as a solo mum. She set the example for us about what it meant to 'become a benefit' to others.

In our family home in Kelston, I remember her sewing early in the mornings and finishing late in the evenings to make ends meet for us. All my siblings and I who were old enough took turns before and after school to work the sewing machines in order to help out. I can recall having some really fun times with my family as we all chipped in around the sewing machines doing our fair share. This was a regular occurrence for at least eight years after my father passed away in 1981.

Despite our financial difficulties, my mum always showed us that we could still have love and always have the 'Island smile'. Mum used to take pride in making sure the world outside didn't see the poverty we were experiencing. Before we left home she used to take out the baby oil and apply it over our bodies and hair to ensure we all looked smart.

> You may be living in poverty
> but don't ever let poverty live in you.

Unbeknown to my mum, after dad died she would have been entitled to assistance from the government. Having arrived from Samoa, she was not accustomed with the New Zealand social service policies. So the thought of receiving money from the government never crossed her mind. It was only much later on that she was informed of this. By then our hard financial times had passed and most of my siblings and I were grown up and able to take care of ourselves and our family's needs.

On one of my return trips to New Zealand, while I was playing for Newcastle, I remember visiting mum and seeing a letter from a finance company congratulating her for finally paying off her loan with them. I enquired as to what Mum had used the loan for. After much persuasion, she told me that it was for the $2000 I needed when I toured Japan in 1987 with the New Zealand Schools team.

I had been under the impression that it was from contributions by our extended family, but my assumption was incorrect. By making the sacrifice and giving me the chance to make that tour, she allowed the door for my future successes to stay open. I am always and forever grateful to my mum for all she has done for us – and more so for the role model she is.

So breaking the mindset of perpetually having a hand out for a handout or going 'cap in hand' to the government is what I want to see stopped in my people. They need to be equipped with fishing rods to feed themselves rather than be content to receive fish thrown out by others. I was heard on national TV last year making the comment that it was high time that Pacific Islanders began owning the factories that they were working in rather than just being content working there. Thomas Jefferson, third President of the United States of America and principal author of the Declaration of Independence, put it this way:

The democracy will cease to exist when you take away from those who are willing to work and give to those who would not.

Yes, I know that the stand I'm taking here can be construed as controversial, but I am entitled to my opinion. That's the beauty of living in a democracy. I believe that the facts need to speak for themselves as it seems to me that our people are on a downward spiral. Currently when you look at where Pacific Islanders sit in New Zealand in regard to health, education, crime, youth, there are major problems. A lot of people would like me to ignore these issues and be politically correct. Well, I am not like that and I want to expose these areas so that the real issues can be attended to. Perhaps my people aren't directed by statistics. Maybe they don't want to know. But I say they need to know for the future welfare of their families and the generations to come. The onus is upon us to remedy these situations and I believe it starts at home. This is my personal view.

Sure, it is easy for me to sit back and do nothing, but that's not what I was brought up to do. However, I can't make a huge difference on my own and that is why I encourage my people to join with me to tackle these serious matters; to help me untangle all the red tape that bureaucrats weave around us. Thankfully,

I am not a one-man band on this quest. I acknowledge the similar stand Michael Jones has made for family and justice. Like me, he too desires to see our young people aspire and achieve truly great things.

11.

My Better Half

Don't criticise your wife's judgement –
look who she married.

Unknown

This book is dedicated foremost to my wife, Daphne, and my children, so it would be a huge disservice if I didn't pay her the tribute of making a contribution. I thank God for Daphne, whom I love dearly. She has been the rock that I can always rely on for support, my pillar of strength through the various highs and lows, all along the journey from New Zealand to England and back home again.

Sometimes we men can overshadow our women because of our physical dominance. This may tend to soften the voices of our wives. That is so wrong. It is our duty as the man to love our wife, and in my opinion often our wives are not getting the recognition they deserve. There is a quote from the American poet Ralph Waldo Emerson which I think encapsulates the tremendous contribution made by women to society:

'I have thought a sufficient measure of civilization
is the influence of good women.'

I thank God for the two women that have had the most influence in my life – my mum and Daphne. There is no doubt in my mind that they are the unsung heroes of my life story and largely responsible for all I have achieved.

For Daphne, leaving behind the support of close-knit family to accompany her husband to a foreign land was extremely challenging. I cannot profess to fully understand all that she was going through at the time. While I can describe my on-field trials reasonably well, it is Daphne who is best suited to describe to you the challenges we faced as a family along our shared life journey. So without further ado, I will hand you over to my 'better half'.

Daphne Tuigamala
Inga's 'better half'

'That's Inga for you – always a man with a big heart.'

'When I look back to that time when we left New Zealand in 1994 it seems surreal, almost like we hadn't done it. Sometimes I ask myself, "Did we really live overseas for so long, nine years?" Wow! Now we've been back for seven years it doesn't feel as if we lived abroad at all.

'Inga has described to you how during the time before our move to Wigan, we were living in his mum's garage. Now,

I am sure you will agree with me that a garage was not a suitable place in which to bring up our two young sons. On top of that, Inga was also struggling to hold down a full-time job as no one was keen to employ somebody who travelled away so often. Despite these adverse circumstances, when the big-money contracts came knocking we didn't just grab them. Inga and I spoke to many people and sought their advice before we made our decision. When we did finally decide to accept the Wigan offer we sincerely believed that we had made a well-informed one. In hindsight we most certainly did!

'I remember well the day of our departure. In fact, so many people had turned up to see us off that the airport staff had to allocate us a private room. We were also so late for boarding our flight that they had to make a special announcement for us to please go to the boarding gates. It was a mad scramble as we hurried along through customs with both kids in tow. What a relief it was to finally just sit back and relax on the plane.

'The first people to meet us on arrival in Manchester were the Wigan coach and his wife, John and Linda Dorahy, who had come to fetch us. One of the first questions I remember Linda asking us was, "Where are your coats?" In all the rush of emotions we experienced before leaving New Zealand it had totally slipped our minds that we were arriving in England in the middle of winter. Experiencing the full brunt of an English winter was a rude awakening to the system. The place was absolutely freezing!

'I really took pity on my husband in those early days. Before we left New Zealand, Inga had undertaken a national tour to promote his first book, *Inga the Winger*. Consequently, he had not done much training and was nowhere near where he needed to be in terms of his fitness. Add to this the fact that he went straight into training in the bitter cold of winter and you can understand how tough it was for him to make the adjustment. In the early days he would come back from the training sessions pretty sore as he got accustomed to the harder routines.

'More than just the physical battering he was taking, he also had to deal with not having all his wider family around him. It was no surprise that he asked his best friend, Afi, to accompany us to Wigan for a short stay. It was Afi whose car we used on our first date, and in a strange turn of events we later found out that he was my neighbour from Tonga. Afi was a real clown, and always kept us laughing with his antics. Later he went on to play for Wigan's Super League rivals St Helens and his "short stay" with us ended up stretching to about three years.

'Although I had left my birth land, Tonga, at fourteen to live with my aunt in Auckland, so was accustomed to being away from friends and family, I do admit it was tough for the both of us being so far away. Our phone bill that first year bore testimony to how hard it was for us to adapt to life in our new country. Even though it was tough going when we arrived, I could always count on Inga for his support. Together we relied on each other to pull through, which we did. Linda Dorahy was fantastic too, taking me around to meet the players' wives and helping me adjust to life in Wigan. Altogether, it probably took about two years to settle down to our new life and really get accustomed to the climate.

'On the social side of things, we had too much going on with the kids to worry about the after-match functions. Plus there was the fact that Inga doesn't take alcohol, which was a feature of most of them. However, I really enjoyed it when we used to travel with the team for Inga's away games for Wigan. It was great for Inga too as he loved having us around, and I am sure it was something that the rest of the team appreciated as well. Buses were hired to take us to some of the best sporting venues in the world: Twickenham, Wembley and many more. Wigan didn't hold back and provided the kids with rugby jerseys sporting the club's famous red and white colours. It was also an ideal opportunity to bond with the other wives and kids.

'Our eldest son Jordan's first day at preschool is one I remember vividly. As he was always around Inga's mum and family in New Zealand he mainly spoke Samoan. That was the one "small" bit of information I forgot to tell his teacher who couldn't make head or tail of him. Inga and I had a good chuckle about it at the time, but it didn't take Jordan long to start speaking English. Not just any type of English though – English with a proper English accent! Later on, when Inga was on loan to Wasps in London for six months, it was even more amusing to have our kids return from school and start calling the toilets "lavatories". And even more amusing when they started asking for permission to leave the dinner table – something we didn't ever do before.

'Not long after our arrival, Henry Paul also came over with his wife to play for Wigan. About six months later, Inga's cousin Apollo Perelini, who had played for North Harbour, came to play for rivals St Helens. Inga's younger brother Lua also turned up for a holiday but ended up liking the place so much that he stayed on. I soon found myself adopting the role of showing the "newbies" around and introducing them to others.

'It was during Inga's six-month loan spell with London-based Wasps that our daughter, Salote, was born. (Queen Salote of Tonga is especially remembered for honouring Queen Elizabeth by refusing to use an umbrella in the rain at the English monarch's coronation.) The move to Wasps ultimately led to Inga being offered a contract with Newcastle, where we spent five years in beautiful North East England. Just as in Wigan, we were well received in Newcastle, and it was here that we were able to renew our ties with Pat Lam and his family who was also offered a contract with them. Their kids and ours were around the same age and we enjoyed having them there. At Newcastle our house was always full, and it was in this town that our youngest son, Silika, was born.

'It was unusual at that time to find many Pacific Islanders living in England but we were in for a pleasant surprise as our home very quickly became the "United Nations of the Pacific Islands in England". After one particular game Inga was approached by two teenage Tongan boys, Epeli Taione and Soakai Manukia, and invited them over for dinner as they were homesick. That's Inga for you – always a man with a big heart. He convinced Newcastle to give them a trial who were so impressed by their performance they very soon offered them a playing contract. Not having a place to stay at first, they lived with us for a while and I had a house full of men to cook for. From what I hear, Epeli has gone on to great feats with the Tongan national rugby team at various world cups but sadly Soa has passed away. After another of his games Inga was approached by a Samoan pastor who had been living in Newcastle for a good few years. He and his kids – who despite looking Samoan, were amazingly English-sounding – quickly became part of our extended family. Then there were our Tongan friends, the doctors Viliami and Aivi Puloka.

'With so many of us around we decided to bring a little bit of the Pacific Islands to England. So for a few Christmases we had an Island theme with the traditional "pig on a spit" under a marquee at our place in the cold English winter. Our neighbours indoors with their traditional turkey probably thought we were mad. Eventually, word got round, and attendance at our Christmas gatherings grew so large we had to move to a local hall to cater for everybody. There was no holding back at these parties where we had bouncy castles and face painting, and at one of them Inga got an English colleague of his to play Santa – the poor guy had a nightmare trying to pronounce all the Island kids' names!'

RETURN TO NEW ZEALAND

'Towards the end of 2001, Inga was really starting to feel the effects of playing non-stop rugby. His body wasn't recovering as quickly as before from the knocks and injuries he sustained. Also, he had earned a good rest from the game and was happy to retire. Whilst we had enjoyed our time in the northern hemisphere, we knew that we wanted our kids to appreciate their roots and culture back in New Zealand. In England our kids used to call all our friends "aunty and uncle" but when they returned to New Zealand they couldn't believe how they were now calling their actual relatives by these names. There was no more "pretend family" like in England.

'As Inga has told you, staying at home was not the ideal situation for me and pretty soon I got bored so started to work at a local café in West Auckland. The café scene was so enjoyable that in 2003 Inga and I decided to start up our own. It was fun while it lasted but the pressures of this work eventually took their toll. I had to leave home early to open up and do the preparation for the day which meant I missed the kids in the mornings. Inga used to drop them at school and pick them up as well whilst I closed the shop. Two years of this lifestyle was enough and we sold it in 2005.

'The first year of Inga's new calling as a funeral director was tough going. In the beginning it was just Inga and I managing pretty much the entire operation by ourselves. Now I can confidently say that we are on top of things and enjoy serving our community through our business. As parents we also enjoy the flexibility that this work offers us as it allows us to spend more time with our kids. We get to leave home with them now and I am able to pick them up from school as well. People who work for themselves will agree that while it is hard work owning your own business the rewards are great.'

MY TRIBUTE TO INGA

'In writing this contribution to Inga's book I want to say that a huge part of his success in life is derived from honouring God. He understands his role in God's eyes as husband and father by always putting me and the kids at the forefront of all his decisions. We are always included in his plans and he tries to take us everywhere he goes. At times the kids will moan a little about getting dragged along but they realise it is because he enjoys us being with him so much. They really love their dad for always making time for them as they know that with the busy lives we lead it can become all too easy not to make the time. It is important for our children to see that we are supportive of each other and my heartfelt advice to all other parents is to:

- Spend quality time with your kids.

- Always enjoy and appreciate that time you spend with your kids.

- Do it now as it's too late when they're grown up.

'Over the years I have come to appreciate that more than being my husband, the father to my kids and a leader to our extended family, Inga has been blessed with a much larger role to play with respect to the wider community whom he has adopted. Inga is humbled by the opportunity rugby has given him to be able to influence people and has always counted it a privilege. This is why you will always find him making time for everyone whenever he can. As his wife I stand by him and support him in this role to fulfil his larger calling in life.'

While I am grateful to my wife for paying me such a glowing tribute, it is to her that the true acclaim is owed. She has been very gracious in what she has said, but there is a side of me that has been hidden. Just like everybody else, what seems nice in the public eye isn't always everything that its cracked up to be. Thus far, all you have heard are the good things about me, my achievements and accolades. However, there is more that needs to be added for you to get to know the true Inga Tuigamala.

Good relationships are never founded on a one-way basis. It can be easy for the male to dominate in a relationship, and perhaps losing my father young is the reason I almost got it all so wrong later on in my marriage. Yes, I had my older brothers and uncles, but it was not the same as having a father around to be a role model to follow. Daphne and I met each other when we were teenagers – meaning that she's been around me for a long time. To be honest, I truly don't know how she's put up with me for so long. All my triumphs have been based on the faithfulness, patience and perseverance with which she has held our marriage together. Yet it was these very successes of mine that I was using to shut my wife up with, and not give her the opportunity to fully express either herself or her opinions.

This continuous erring on my part resulted in a rude awakening for me in 2004. It was a time when we were still settling back into life in New Zealand and I was finding my feet in 'retirement'. With all that was going on I confess I dropped the ball in my relationship with my wife. At the time I was oblivious to the huge cracks that were starting to appear in our marriage because I was so consumed with myself and doing the things that *I* wanted to do. My world came crashing down when I received a note from Daphne in my office telling me she needed some time away from me with the children so that she could clear her head. At first I thought she was joking – after all, wasn't I providing her a lifestyle that many women would enjoy?

I wasn't used to returning to an empty house with no children running up to jump all over me as they usually did. As the night grew longer and I sat there all alone it was a real torture for me and I couldn't take it. All that I strived for in my life was my family. Those who knew me saw that I always placed them as my priority in all that I did. So where had I gone wrong? Eventually it dawned on me I had made myself believe a lie that I was being a great husband in providing my wife with all the material things of this world – the houses, cars, holidays, jewellery – when what I was really doing was using the wealth I had accumulated over the years to shut her up. It was always me having the last say on matters that was really shattering her. I had the attitude that as the head of the household it was my right to do whatever I wanted to. Through this dumb attitude I almost lost everything that really mattered to me. No winning try, medals, man of the match awards, money, houses, flash cars or jewellery could compensate for the bitter knowledge that I had let my wife and my children down.

Fortunately, Daphne and I were able to sit down and with the guidance and advice of our pastor work through a lot of issues. We were able to strip everything back in order to get to the root of the problem. Over the years I had allowed my marriage to develop a gaping wound that needed more than a band-aid to patch it up. A major part of our healing came from me admitting that I had got things wrong. The blame rested solely with me and nobody else. After talking to Daphne and having her share all that was in her heart, I felt like a real ogre. My problem had been that in the past I used to *hear* her but not *listen* to her. I did try to make changes but they were just superficial ones, done more to please her than as a way of dealing with the real underlying issues.

By having things my own way all the time I was not giving my wife the room to grow and I was definitely not respecting her views or being sensitive to her needs in our marriage. Here I was being a mentor, father figure and friend to all the other people in my life but to my own wife I was being a taskmaster. Before I eagerly leapt in to help someone else I needed to make sure that my own house was in order first. Thankfully, there was no third party involved in our problem and it was just me that needed to get my act together. Through this whole experience, I learnt a very important truth:

> If the man wants to be treated like a king
> in his house then he needs to make sure
> that he treats his wife as a queen.

The reason I have shared this unflattering side of my life is because I want other men to sit up and take notice as I believe there are many women out there suffering in silence like my wife did. I want men to be exposed to the harsh reality that we can mess things up pretty bad if we are not staying in touch with our wives' feelings and their needs. Our wives are not just there to cook the dinner and look after the kids. I got that very wrong and I was shown up for my shortcomings.

> They say that experience is a hard teacher because
> she gives the test first and the lesson afterwards.

In life as well as sport, the reality is that we learn more from our losses than our wins. When Daphne and I look back together at that time we see that it was the beginning of a much better marriage for us. Let me spell out what I learnt in order to make it clearer:

- I was too dominant and wanted everything done *my* way.
- I was more confident in the material things that I was

providing and assumed that was all that mattered.

- I was shutting Daphne out of the decision-making process.
- I had to show Daphne how I valued her by trusting her judgement.
- A happy partnership is based on two people making good decisions.
- One of the main lessons in relationships is that it is a two-way street.
- Marriage is certainly for the mature, not the immature.

I have found in this day and age that the trend of not trying hard enough is quite acceptable. In general, modern society promotes and accepts the attitude that if things get a tad difficult then it is okay to quit without making a sincere attempt to rectify the situation. Take the prevalent high rates of divorce. Don't get me wrong, I'm not talking about divorce for reasons of abuse or infidelity, but the situations where it becomes 'inconvenient' to remain married. Rather than working out their differences, couples choose the easy option of divorce. And we all know who the ones are that suffer the most – the children!

Differences between a husband and wife will always crop up at times – Daphne and I experience them as well. We choose to work through them. My advice is to put your hand up for help. Speak to your elders or other married couples that you respect. Remember that you are never alone. It's always easy to throw in the towel, but that should not be the option to take without seeking help first. When help arrives, be prepared to accept it and to listen and act on the advice as well. Luckily for us, Daphne and I had people who we could go to and get great advice.

An important lesson I learnt from participating in the 4 x 100 metre relay in my days at Kelston Boys' High School was 'don't drop the baton'. You have to focus on handing it over securely to your team-mate in order to ensure success in crossing the finish line. I believe that life is pretty much like a relay race. The previous generation has a responsibility to hand down to the generations after them the 'baton' of the good virtues that have been instilled in them. Marriage is one of them and has proved to be the fundamental foundation of any decent society. My advice to married couples is to cherish their marriage by honouring their vows. Guys, this precept will sound cheesy but it is so true:

Happy wife = happy life.

Deliberating over what my concluding words to you on this topic would be, it came to me as I read a message entitled

'Wait no longer, speak!'

from our family daily devotional reading, *The Word for Today*. What I took on board from this message is what I have come to see as the problem with many people. They wait too long because they are hesitant, neither here nor there. As a result, they miss out on ideal opportunities.

Take the example of double amputee Mark Inglis whom I had the pleasure of meeting recently. Recounting his remarkable trip up Everest, he especially captivated me with his account of stepping into 'The Death Zone', above 8000 metres on Everest where with temperatures around minus 50 degrees Celsius you either keep moving or you'll die – there is normally a window of just five to fifteen days to make a bid for the summit, so planning is crucial. One out of every fourteen climbers fails in the attempt. (Wow! In my rugby days, the worst consequence of making a mistake in our play may have been a penalty against us or even a try, not loss of life.) It occurred to me that every relationship has a similar 'window' or timeframe in which it is apt for us to act, especially when we get things wrong and need to make amends. In order for our relationships to survive we have to act. We miss out on the greater rewards that life has to offer if we procrastinate.

Something else we need to contemplate is the power of the spoken word. Many times I have cut down my wife and children with my tongue and was totally ashamed of myself afterward. Just as the wrong words make us remorseful, the right words spoken at the right time are incredibly powerful. Yet if they are not spoken within this 'right time' it can become a heavy burden to live with. The following passage from *The Word for Today* really gave me food for thought:

- I remember when I took your new car on the road and wrecked it. I thought you'd be livid and come down hard on me, but you didn't.
- I remember when we went to the beach and you didn't want to go because you said it was going to rain. We went and it rained. I was sure you'd rub it

in and say, 'I told you so!' But you didn't.

- Then there was the time when I spilled blueberry juice down the front of your new white tux. I knew you'd be upset and blame me. But you didn't.
- And remember that formal evening? I was mistaken and told you it was casual. You wore blue jeans and felt like a fish out of water. I was sure you would storm out in anger and leave me standing there. But you didn't.
- I wanted to tell you how much I loved you and how much I appreciated you for all those things when you returned from Vietnam. But you didn't.

We take for granted the time that we have with each other. As a funeral director I see the reality of how fragile and precious life is. Why live the rest of your life in regret and bearing within you those unspoken words that can set you or the person they are intended for free? What guarantee do we have that we will be able to see that person again and have the chance to say it to them? In my current line of work I'm frequently amazed at the wonderful floral arrangements I see adorning coffins or gravesides. But I often think

it is good to give flowers when people die,
but even better to give them while people are alive
and can appreciate it.

When was the last time you gave your wife a bouquet of flowers? When was the last time you treated your loved one to something special? Don't leave it to tomorrow, for tomorrow may never come. Common words that I hear at funerals are 'if only'. If only I had done this or that, things would have turned out differently. Remember we are on planet Earth for a brief time, so live your life with no regrets. If there is one message that I want you to take away from reading my book it is this thought from Goethe:

> 'Things which matter most must never be
> at the mercy of things which matter least.'

Let's face it, how many people have you heard of who on their deathbeds wish they'd spent more time at the office? Or ask for their cheque books, bank statements, cell phones or laptops to embrace and comfort them? Don't wait till your deathbed to enjoy being around your family. Don't be a fool and leave it too late. If there are some changes you need to start making, then start making them now. Don't put it off until it's too late. My greatest priorities in life are to always be improving in my relationship with God, my wife and my children. The rest is secondary. It is my hope that this book is a help to you as you journey through life. God bless you!

Afterword

I am sure you will be in agreement with me when I say, 'What an amazing book!' I applaud Inga for being so candid and transparent in what he has shared in these pages. I am confident that it will be useful to us and that we can learn from the many lessons he has shared. Although so much has already been said by Inga and about Inga, I still have some more to add.

What really stands out for me about Inga Tuigamala – and something I had always seen in him – was his leadership potential. He may not admit to it, but he was one of the most articulate and smartest team-mates that I have known. Murray Deaker alluded to his intelligence in the foreword but Inga tries hard to mask it with his happy-go-lucky persona and plays the funny hard-case Island boy with his cheeky grin. In fact, as I am sure you will acknowledge after reading to this point, he is actually a deep thinker and a very wise individual. He is not just filled with head knowledge either, but is what some would call 'street smart', or as he puts it, a student of the 'university of life'.

Inga is also a man who possesses great charisma. He has the ability to enter any room and automatically draw people to him. There are not many individuals I know with his capacity to break down people's facades and have them warm to him straight away – I certainly can't do that. He is a gift to the Pacific and his ability to cross over between so many cultures is a real blessing. Amongst his many other talents he speaks fluent Tongan and Samoan (the Tongans like to claim him as their own as Inga has a bit of Tongan heritage as well). Even here in New Zealand with its pretty diverse cultural tapestry he is able to break down a lot of divides and stereotypes to occupy a unique space and place in our society. Inga is at his ease anywhere in New Zealand, whether it is walking through the Otara markets in South Auckland, strolling through the upmarket streets of Parnell, attending a school gala in Invercargill at the bottom of the South Island, or having an orange juice at the local pub up north in Kaitaia. That's Inga, the man with the charm and charisma to relate to and get on with all types of people.

In the rugby world I was one of the few who knew about Inga's double life when he played for the All Blacks. The majority of people would not have known about the sad state of his financial affairs in those days. As an All Black at the time you were living the dream and flying high, but every night Inga came back to the reality of sleeping in the garage at the back of his mum's house with Daphne and little Jordan. In fact, a lot of us Pacific Island rugby players in those early days lived simple, very basic lives, in most cases still staying with our parents. Inga and Daphne did have it pretty tough, so it was great that people like Kevin Roberts of Pepsi went out of their way to make his life a bit more comfortable and befitting of an All Black. When Inga left to take up his league contract with Wigan he was still maturing as a young man. He returned from England this amazingly mature well-rounded professional individual in every aspect of his life. Without a doubt, the move to England was the best thing that could have ever happened for him and his family.

My earliest recollection of Inga is hearing about this sixteen- or seventeen-year-old rugby sensation that played on the wing for Kelston Boys High. Being four years older than Inga, by that time I was playing senior rugby for Auckland and I think that I had made the All Blacks as well. However, I was enraged to hear all the talk about some snotty-nosed kid from Kelston being hailed as the next BG Williams. Being both Samoan and an All Black, as well as bright and intelligent, Bryan Williams was a hero to our generation of Polynesians and there could be no one like him. BG was the man!

Eventually my chance to 'welcome' this upstart to the big time by smashing him came in a clash between Waitemata and Ponsonby, our respective clubs. The ball came off a ruck and Inga took it at pace. Tackling is all about timing, so I was lining him up on my radar and waiting for that right moment to launch. I was like a jet-fighter pilot waiting for the 'missile lock' function to start beeping on my screen to confirm that the target was ready to be shot down. I thought that I had him too, as 99.99 per cent of the time when I launched I couldn't miss. All I remember is diving and Inga producing this unbelievable left-foot sidestep that had me clutching fresh air. One minute the big guy was coming at me and I was licking my lips in anticipation of this massive hit I was going to put on him, and the next minute he was gone! Much to the glee of the Ponsonby supporters, I ended up looking like a right idiot in front of the Waitemata faithful. Inga went on to dance past three of our other guys and score under the posts in that play.

Not surprisingly, due to his prodigious talent Inga had been rushed straight into senior rugby when he left secondary school. Now I knew first-hand that this guy was a star in the making – and the rest, as they say, is history. Inga went on to make the Auckland team quickly and we hit it off straight away simply because we had so much in common including:

- Our shared Samoan heritage.
- Growing up in the same suburb.
- Being raised by strong mums.
- Both losing our fathers when we were quite young.
- The caring support of an extended family.
- A love for God.

As you can see, it was quite evident that our stories were similar and it was our faith that was the real glue of our friendship more than anything else. For me to see this young man turn the world upside down playing for Auckland and then the All Blacks at the 1991 World Cup was special. I found it hard being a young shy Polynesian kid going into the All Blacks' world, so I could empathise with Inga's plight. He had to break a lot more ground than I did, especially being a full Samoan with a less pronounceable name to mainstream New Zealanders. I really admired him for achieving this milestone. He took his place among the Joneses, Stanleys, Schusters, Williamses, and way back the Solomons, in the proud list of Pacific Island All Blacks.

Like me, you will have been blown away after reading Inga's account of his life journey. Lesser mortals would have chosen to stay home in the comforts of New Zealand and union. That's what I did! I can relate to some of the hard lessons he learned along the way as a father, husband and someone that would like to contribute to the world. Potentially, this last ambition is achieved at the expense of our own families, which are the reality of the passion we share for our fellow people and for our communities. We both have particular concerns for the welfare of the most vulnerable – particularly Pacific youth, who are infamously known as 'the long brown tail' of New Zealand society. As Inga has rightly mentioned, the sorry state of affairs of our people in most of the statistics is that we are right at the bottom. Inga understands the importance of being at the head and not the tail, which is something he attributes to learning from my mum, and which she actually learnt from the Bible.

My mum always cast a conscience vote for whoever she felt would best represent her values, and I have inherited that approach from her. Inga and I were both brought up to believe that if another person could make it ahead in life, then so could we. Neither of us was taught to believe in dependency thinking that is all about making excuses or blaming others for our lot in life – 'excuse-itis, blame-itis, victim-itis' is what I prefer to call the sickness of this mindset. We want people to take responsibility for their lives, always remembering that people are limited not by their place of birth or the colour of their skin, but by the size of their hope.

That's why even at a national level I see Inga as having a really significant role to play in this country's future direction. Together we have made a stand for the National Party in New Zealand which has really set the cat amongst the pigeons. Sure, we knew our decision was going to draw criticism from certain sectors of the population. However, what we saw in the previous political leadership were values that didn't adequately represent Pacific Islanders and those things to which we hold true. Therefore, it was not a difficult call for us to make as we wanted to stay true to who we were and what we were taught by our parents. If our people are to be at the head and not the tail we have to do things differently and try and position ourselves for success.

Inga and I still support each other to this day – just like we did when we were on the rugby field. Back then it was our battlefield and Inga was one of the guys that I knew would be prepared to 'die' for me on the field. There aren't many players that I could honestly say would do that. We back each other up on many issues and matters that we have to take a stand for in our public life too. As brothers we stand together because we are driven and motivated by the same values.

At present we are involved with a sports academy and community gym, which we see as vehicles to re-engage young men back into education and life, using their sports abilities. Through these initiatives we want to maximise their potential. We want to take those young men and place them among the people, infrastructure, programmes and resources to help them fulfil their potential – whether that is to play for the Warriors, Blues or All Blacks, or even one day own their own business or go on to other tertiary training.

It's a well-known adage that it takes a village to raise a child, and both of us are the product of being raised by a village of people who cared for us after we lost our dads at a young age. Having a village philosophy means bringing all the right people together to invest in young people and nurture them to be the best they can possibly be and live out their aspirations. Consequently, this belief in the value of village lies at the heart of our shared mission.

My friendship with Inga is something I cherish, and I know that he will be there for me at the drop of a hat if I need him. Not only is he a wonderful gift to me but to so many others. Take it from someone who has been close to Inga for such a long time, I think I really know the key to his success in life, both on and off the field. I believe Inga's secret is captured in this Samoan proverb:

'O le ala o le pule o le tautua.'

It means:

'The road to true leadership
is through servanthood.'

Inga has developed into a true leader only because he has spent his life serving others. Therefore he can rightfully take his place as a leader in society.

When we esteem others and consider their needs, the Bible says that we are displaying the 'attitude of Christ'. It was because of this servant attitude that Christ was exalted to be above everything, and to it I attribute Inga's tremendous success and favour with people. Too many people these days are busy looking out for 'number one'. When we consider the needs of others we can all make this a better world. Like my good friend Va'aiga Tuigamala, we would do well to keep in mind the Bible's wise counsel that

'the way to the king's chambers
is through the servants' quarters'.

I thank Inga for having given me the opportunity to share with you this 'last word'. However, I'm sure he would be in agreement with me that the person who should really have the afterword in our lives is our Lord and Saviour Jesus Christ:

'Whoever would be great among you
must first become your servant.'

God bless,
Michael Jones
All Black, 1987–98

Acknowledgements

There are a lot of people to thank. So let me start off first with my better half, my rock, my best friend and my darling wife, Daphne. You have stuck with me all through the good and the bad times. Thanks for being so loyal to me. All of my accomplishments would not have been possible without you.

To my hero, my mum, Mrs Fa'atauala Pulelua Lealuga Fesolai Tuigamala. Thank you for all your sacrifices and the unconditional love you have shown towards all of us.

To my eldest child, Jordan, for his part in this book, thank you son. Interestingly, we open the book with his words, before contributing further with his take on how he sees me towards the end.

Sincere thanks to Murray Deaker, for his straight-talking, no-nonsense comments and honesty in the Foreword.

Kevin Roberts, thank you for giving me the opportunity in

1993 at Pepsi and remaining a faithful friend and mentor.

Special thanks to the following great friends for taking the time from their busy schedules to contribute to my book and sharing their experiences of me. I am honoured to have been associated with you all: Apollo Perelini, Jack Robinson, Jason Robinson, Rob Andrew, Jonny Wilkinson, To'o Vaega, Martin Offiah and Pat Lam.

Thanks to John and Ann Strickland, for their friendship in our early days settling into life in Wigan. Thanks again to John for his hospitality and assistance to Myan Subrayan in his travels in England researching for this book.

To my longtime friend, whom I admire and respect, Michael Jones. Thanks for the Afterword. You are an inspirational community leader, husband, father and a true friend.

To my author, good friend and brother in Christ, Myan Subrayan. I believed you were the right person to convey my words into a book I could proudly put my name to. Thanks for helping me tell my life story the way that I wanted it to be told.

To God, be the glory for the great things He has done and still to do!

Addressing parents of Pretoria Noord High School at Pre- Winter Sports Event

Team talk to Cheetahs Rugby

Sharks team Talk

Speaker at Biotronik sales and Marketing conference 2015

With Chad Le Clos at King Shaka airport press conference Durban

Life coaching the Lions

Springboks in Dublin 2014

All Black 7's Team Talk

Maritzburg Utd Team talk

MYAN SUBRAYAN

Life Coach, Speaker and Writer

Myan Subrayan resides in Pretoria since 2012, where he is a business advisor, speaker, writer, and works with elite sportsmen & professional teams as a life coach. He has written:
- Olympic gold medallist swimmer, Chad Le Clos' first book, Unbelievable,
- Current Springbok and Bulls captain, Pierre Spies: More than Rugby,
- Former Springbok, Jannie de Beer, High Five,
- Former All Black, Inga Tuigamala's Inga: My Story.

Currently he is writing former Bafana Bafana player Delron Buckley's book.

Motivation

- For businesses: leadership, management, sales, customer service, teamwork, change management
- Sports: Individuals, teams, coaches and management
- Schools: Students and teachers,

Life Coaching

- Focus on discovering your values, purpose and aligning and putting them into Acton, adopting an overall, holistic approach to coaching the whole person,
- Work towards goal setting to create a better future and life today,
- Help take responsibility and to maximize your own potential.
- Tailored sessions for individual or teams

Myan's Focus

He is a change expert aiding in the process of self-discovery which allows individuals to move forward with confidence in what they do.

Conclusion

The ability to maintain focus, control emotions and perform under pressure is the difference between winning and losing. Myan is aware of this and targets his sessions to encompass all of these above.

For more info visit www.myansubrayan.co.za or email myan@myansubrayan.com
Tel: 081 271 2242

You can also follow him on Twitter & Facebook.

Springboks in Dublin 2014

Daniel Conference Moreleta

" Having heard Myan speak on a few occasions, his passion and humour are refreshing and keep his listeners interested " - Patrick Lambie (Sharks/Springbok)